LEFT TO WRITE TOO

Second Edition

Developing Effective
Written Language Programmes
for Young Learners

Harry Hood

dunmore press

Acknowledgements: The following are acknowledged and thanked for allowing the use of samples of their work:
Edmonton School (Auckland)
Glen Eden Intermediate (Auckland)
Gore Main School (Southland)
Gorge Road School (Southland)
Henley School (Nelson)
Invercargill North School
Invercargill South School
Kenmure Intermediate (Dunedin)
Lumsden School (Southland)
Peterhead School (Hastings)
Salford School (Invercargill)
St. Patrick's School (Invercargill)
Waihopai School (Invercargill)
Waikiwi School (Invercargill)

NEMP Writing Committee: Dr Peter Crooks and Lester Flocton
Teachers and Children: Abbotsford School Dunedin
Jo Knight, Marketing Manager, Dunedin College of Education
Russell Garbutt, photographs

Left to Write, first edition published in 1995.
Left to Write Too, is a revised and expanded version of that publication.

Second Edition: ISBN 0 86469 364 8

© 2000 Harry Hood
© 2000 Dunmore Press Ltd

Dunmore Press Ltd
P.O. Box 5115
Palmerston North
New Zealand
Ph: (06) 358 7169
Fax: (06) 357 9242
Email: dunmore@xtra.co.nz

Australian Supplier:
Federation Press
P.O. Box 45
Annandale 2038 NSW
Australia
Ph: (02) 9552 2200
Fax: (02) 9552 1681

Left to Write Too was first published in 1997 by Berkley Curriculum Publishing

All rights reserved. No part of this publication may be reproduced, stored in a retrieval system, or transmitted in any form or by means, electronic, mechanical, photocopying, recording or otherwise without permission in writing from the publisher.

Contents

Introduction
Our mix of teaching philosophies • The importance of whole-school development •
A philosophy for teaching writing • Process writing • Present beliefs   **4**

Chapter 1: Language Teaching or Language Learning?
The reading-writing link • A broad front approach • The importance of experience   **11**

Chapter 2: Emerging As a Writer
The influence of parents on beginning writers • Observing the new entrant • Writing programmes for juniors • The five specifics of writing • 'Talk written down' • Activities that help and hinder learning • Revision • Junior class children and the curriculum • The role of the teacher   **18**

Chapter 3: Why the Fuss About Genre?
The issues • Middle school programmes • Writing across the curriculum • Using the curriculum • Retaining the best aspects of process writing • Writing and close reading • A planned method of genre development • A plan of work for Years Four to Six • School Review: Questions to Ask   **33**

Chapter 4: Shared and Guided Writing
Developing a balanced writing programme • Shared and guided reading and writing • Shared writing • Guided writing • Guided reading and writing: comprehension and meaning • Writing a report   **48**

Chapter 5: The Classroom Programme: Leading the Horse to Water
The teacher and the writer • The questioning chain • The writing partner • The group conference • Self-conferencing • Proof-reading and editing • Using the *I Can* lists • Spelling • Publication   **60**

Chapter 6: The Vexing Question of Spelling
The National Educational Monitoring Project • Invented spelling   **71**

Chapter 7: Working with the English Curriculum
The philosophy and effects of curriculum change • The New Zealand English Curriculum • The writing strand • Problems • Assessment and understanding   **80**

Chapter 8: Monitoring the Individual – Assessing the Curriculum
Monitoring the individual • Learning characteristics during three stages of development • A junior school vision • Assessing curriculum programmes • Levels One to Four outcomes   **90**

Chapter 9: The Longest Journey
Conclusions   **110**

Appendix   **113**

Select Bibliography   **114**

INTRODUCTION

In this chapter

- Our mix of teaching philosophies
- The importance of whole-school development
- A philosophy for teaching writing
- Process writing
- Present beliefs

Old Problems – New Directions

In the introduction of *Left to Write*, I wrote that we must be continually revising our opinions or we are professionally dead. Now, with a change of publisher, I have taken the opportunity of yet again revising this text. New developments continue to occur. The *National Educational Monitoring Project (NEMP)* has identified several areas of concern. The place of reading within a sound writing programme is becoming increasingly important, and the work of a range of educators working in the fields of language development, spelling and writing need to be considered.

Dancing with the Pen gave a philosophy, the curriculum gave the content, but where is the method? This is the major problem facing teachers today. How to translate philosophy and content into classroom practice. *Left to Write Too* was written to help teachers along this sometimes difficult path.

Two new chapters were added in *Left to Write Too* and now, in the Second Edition, a new chapter on *Spelling* has been included. Each chapter of this text has been revised in line with current educational thinking.

Our Mix of Teaching Philosophies

The last fifteen years have seen major changes, along with much debate, in the teaching of written language. On one hand, the process teachers have based their programmes around writer control of topic, inventive spelling, the teaching of writing as a process, and the publication of writing for classroom readers. These teachers have built on the work of Donald Graves, whose research excited so much interest in the early 1980s.

On the other hand there are the traditionalists. These teachers believe in what they see as sound, no-nonsense education. Their beliefs are hallmarked by their insistence on setting topics, marking all errors, skills teaching, spelling lists and language drills. They believe strongly that they give their children a sound grounding in the basics of written language.

A third group of teachers has picked out all the organisational orthodoxies of process writing and placed these over the top of their traditional methods. Working this way, without any understanding of either learning philosophy, is unfortunately quite common, and probably quite dangerous. It could be called the 'foot-in-both-camps' theory. It is a shame that most teachers, practical people that they are, seem more interested in the *how* than the *why*. These teachers are so unsure of what they are doing that they are likely to comment, 'We do process writing for six weeks each term.'

There has now appeared a fourth grouping of teachers. These teachers are constrained by school programmes. In their efforts to '*teach*' the new curriculum, they divide their programmes into slots: three weeks of *poetic*, three of *expressive* and three of *transactional* writing. In many cases, the needs of children are not being met: programme therefore becomes more important than children.

Defining the problem

The advent of a new curriculum statement has placed yet another constraint on the way writing programmes are developed. The requirement to have children meet achievement objectives is seeing teachers give children less choice as teachers try, in many cases, to artificially construct learning contexts so that the curriculum objectives can be developed. Often children are being forced into attempting to write in ways that are beyond their developmental level.

Sadly for many children, these conflicting philosophies are too often found within the same staff. I know of instances where children experience great confusion as they move through the school. They experience teachers who try out different teaching methods and have different expectations. Is it any wonder that some become totally confused?

I well remember a teacher coming up to me at the end of an evening seminar say, 'I wish the other two teachers in our department had been here tonight.' When asked why, she continued, 'The teacher next to me demands that everything be correct. The children line up for words, or are expected to look up words as they write. One of my children from last year's class came back to me and said, "Mrs Smith, you taught us wrong." I could have cried.'

It has been said that if teachers believe in their programme students will learn, and this is probably true. New Zealand has always produced a number of intuitive teachers who do wonderful things in the classroom but cannot explain their teaching philosophies. Unfortunately for these teachers, times are changing. Parents and society in general are demanding higher levels of professionalism from teachers, and are now expected to be able to articulate their teaching beliefs.

The Importance of Whole-School Development

Schools can no longer afford to carry the uninformed. In saying this we must remember that schools have a responsibility for the ongoing professional development of their staff. Often this has meant taking part in teacher development programmes. These programmes are designed to give individual teachers opportunity to think through their current classroom practice, learn new ideas and methods and re-define their teaching philosophies.

Current research leads us to believe that these programmes have limited effect over time in producing teacher change. While these courses are still popular with many teachers, they seldom do much to change long-term teacher thinking. The strength of one-off courses is that they allow teachers from a range of schools to share ideas. While many would argue that the demise of these courses would cause the New Zealand school system to become incestuous and that this interchange of ideas between schools and teachers is educationally healthy, we must realise that these courses seldom foster long-term school development.

On the other hand, school development programmes where the total staff engage in common experiences seem to be far more successful in effecting permanent change. All staff go through the same experiences and are expected to support each other. At the end of the day, teachers should feel that they have enough knowledge to contribute to collective decisions as to how school programmes will function.

It is important that the principal is up to date with what is happening in curriculum development. More often than not, teachers go to courses but principals never attend. Yet the principal is surely the professional leader of the school. Are principals that much more aware of current curriculum developments than their teachers?

The focus on set curriculum objectives means that the principal must help staff see a common vision. Breaking the curriculum into levels of achievement while giving some programme direction is not a sound basis on which to set a school vision. A school has to set an overall direction for the programme, and then consider levels of achievement.

Prior to the publication of *Dancing with the Pen*, I used to say in schools, 'You must make up your mind as to what path you follow.' Either all teach in a traditional way or all teach via the process approach. Now I say, 'The great debate is over. *Dancing with the Pen* is the official handbook. You decide how your school delivers the ideas expressed in the text.' I have really enjoyed being able to be so positive.

As authors we wanted to stress the need for schools to develop this consistency of approach. We believed that writing was too important a life skill to allow teachers to follow a variety of opinions and interpretations. We felt that each school needed to develop a sense of vision, a negotiated vision, that all would be expected to follow. We believed that only then would we see a general improvement in the standard of written language teaching.

National monitoring is important because it gives schools an indication of national trends. I have been lucky enough to have been involved as a member of the National Policy Committee, and was given the honour of acting as national spokesperson to comment on the *Writing* report. The committee is strong in the belief that within each school, common visions and procedures are essential if there is to be the hoped for improvement in educational achievement.

This report raises a number of important issues. These include the need to:
- **develop school-wide methods of instruction.**
- **improve spelling and punctuation standards.**
- **develop a better oral language base.**
- **reinforce writing revision strategies.**
- **develop wider audiences – outside of teacher and class.**
- **build on the high approval rating given to the subject by Year Four children.**
- **make sure that narrative is not neglected in the upper class levels.**
- **improve the lot of children working in lower socio-economic areas.**
- **reflect on gender differences and the low achievement of Maori children.**

I will try to address the recommendations of the committee in this text.

A Philosophy for Teaching Writing

I have been working with young writers and their teachers for seventeen years. The first new entrants I worked with are now in their twenties, while some of the seniors are in their thirties. Many of these are currently enrolled at universities, some are married and many have joined the work force. Among the first group that I followed are two teachers, a lawyer, an accountant, two nurses, a farmer, a doctor, two doing postgraduate studies, and several who have married and are now bringing up their own children.

Some of these people are now just names; their faces having dissolved with the passage of time. Some will never be forgotten. I will always remember an eight-year-old girl named Lesley who wanted to take her pet goat along on the family's Christmas holiday. She wanted the goat to have new adventures so that she could write about them on her return to school. Lesley, and others like her, all made statements that said, 'I am a writer.'

Every so often I will pick up one of my first handwritten texts that tried to tell teachers how to teach process writing. I look at these books published in the early 1980s. I read, and say to myself, 'Did I really believe that?' I know that I did at the time. I wrote to give teachers a starting point as they tried to gain information about this new teaching approach called process writing.

I then consider my writings of the mid-1980s. I note a change. My classroom observations and feedback from around the country had indicated that others were not enjoying the same positive outcomes as our southern experiences. My writings during this time show a shift from writing about process writing to discussing the writing process. It had become obvious that process writing, the way many teachers were endeavouring to teach it, was delivering few benefits to New Zealand children. Writing in *Forum (No. 1. 1991)*, I wrote:

> Over the last eight years I have worked with teachers from Auckland to Invercargill. What has continued to strike me is that a large majority of classroom teachers are still ignorant about the philosophy behind 'Process Writing'. Most teachers can talk about their programmes, organisations and methods. They talk freely about 'conferences' and 'publishing' as well as 'invented spelling', but only a small proportion of these teachers can give the logic behind their actions. Much of the teaching is still intuitive. In most cases 'conferencing' is only marking, given a different name, and 'publishing' is seen by many as doing a 'good copy'.[1]

Others, more influential than I, had the same doubts. Ro Griffiths, then head of the Department of Education's Reading and Language Curriculum Division, also had a number of concerns. In 1987 he brought a team together to work on a handbook for teachers. This book became *Dancing with the Pen* (Learning Media, 1991).

Developing a new handbook

Our brief from the Department of Education was to write a teachers' handbook. This handbook was not to promote any particular philosophy of teaching. It was not to be a book about process writing, nor was it to promote creative writing approaches like Elwyn Richardson's methods that were widely used and respected during the 1960s and 1970s.

The new handbook was to study the teaching of writing in a range of contexts. It was expected to promote writing as a tool of learning, carrying on directions set in LARIC[2] It was to be child-centred, and was to focus on teaching students a range of writing strategies in much the same way Dame Marie Clay's research focused on teachers developing reading strategies with learner readers.

Dame Marie's research and her beliefs about how children learn to read were to heavily influence our thinking. Similarly, the work done by Don Holdaway in identifying sound teaching and learning experiences became the cornerstone on which we constructed our text. At the same time we knew we had to have a sound research base to develop our beliefs about how young writers learn to write.

Although there had been a lot of New Zealand material written about teaching children to write, we had to go overseas for current, well researched data. We found that the work done by people such as Graves, Calkins, Gentry, Murray, Wells, Smith, Meek and Cambourne were not at odds with current New Zealand beliefs about language teaching and language learning.[3]

---

1 'Finding the Swan in the Ugly Duckling,' *Reading Forum*. NZ, No. 1, 1991.

2 Later Reading In-service Course. NZ, Department of Education, 1982.

3 It is interesting to compare the 'New Zealand Beliefs About Literacy Learning and Teaching' in *Dancing with the Pen*, pg. 6, with the introduction to *Reading in Junior Classes* pg. 9.

Process Writing

While wanting to produce a text with which New Zealand teachers could feel comfortable, we did not want to lose some of the more stimulating aspects of process writing.

The positive elements of process writing

There were many positive elements that grew out of process writing:
- Children wrote daily.
- New entrant children were expected to take ownership of writing from their first day of school.
- Child ownership of topics produced a sound attitude towards writing.
- Conferences enabled children to discuss writing from a meaning base.
- Invented spelling enabled children to write quickly, and in most cases efficiently.
- Publication enabled less able children to present quality products to their classmates, while more able children developed understandings about the needs of the audience.
- Many teachers improved their questioning techniques. There was a general improvement in the monitoring of individual writers.
- Junior school teachers in particular became more aware of the progressions of writing development.

Concerns about process writing

There were also some concerns that needed to be addressed.
- Some teachers kept old procedures and attached new terms to them.
- Publication was not given enough importance.
- Many times it was just a good copy with a fancy heading.
- Too little time was spent teaching children the routines of conferencing.
- There was often no continuity of instruction through the school.
- Often teachers did not know what they were trying to achieve. Few were given adequate in-service training.
- Few teachers understood invented spelling. Many still insisted on working children through spelling levels.
- The progress of some children seemed to fall away during the Standard Two to Four years (Years Four to Six). In some cases there was less creative or poetic writing undertaken as teachers got caught up in complete child choice of topic.[4]

There were many other aspects of process writing that could be deemed successes or failures, but why delve into the past? It is the present and future with which we must now be concerned.

Present Beliefs

I believe that the Graves research is basically sound, supported as it is by the Australian, Brian Cambourne, when he identifies conditions that encourage language learning.[5] Cambourne's seven conditions are as follows:

4 This is discussed fully in the chapter 'Why the Fuss About Genre?'

5 A full explanation of Cambourne's 'Conditions for Natural Learning' are outlined in *The Whole Story*, Ashton's, 1988.

Some Key Conclusions

Children learn best when they write for real purposes and audiences in a variety of written forms.

Learning is a social activity: writers need readers, and writing conferences teach children to question their writing.

In senior classes, the curriculum needs to drive children's writing.

Junior children should be allowed to develop naturally as writers. Learning to write is a developmental process.

Writing 'workshops' are the best way to learn how to teach writing.

Cambourne's and Grace's research is accurate. Both sit comfortably with current New Zealand beliefs about literacy learning.

Demonstration and modelling are two powerful strategies. Teachers must use a variety of approaches to teach writing.

New Zealand teachers can be world leaders in teaching children to write if they use what they already know about teaching children to read.

- Immersion
- Demonstration
- Expectation
- Approximation
- Responsibility
- Employment
- Feedback

Cambourne believes that these conditions are fundamental to all language learning tasks, and could probably be applied to all forms of learning.

You will note that both Graves and Cambourne put forward similar theories as to how children learn language.[6] This is the important lesson to take out of Graves. No matter what programmes teachers put in place, sound learning conditions must be provided. Writing in *Forum (No. 1. 1991)* I remarked:

> I am sure the method is sound, but if we are to achieve success, all teachers need to understand its philosophy and find teaching strategies that will enable children to develop as writers.

---

[6] See Appendix One. This shows how Graves' research parallels Cambourne's learning theories.

1

In this chapter

- **The reading–writing link**
- **Constructing meaning**
- **Revision – the writer's self-correction**
- **A broad-front approach**
- **The reasons for writing**
- **Reading and writing cues**
- **Thinking and speaking in sentences**
- **Writing behaviours**

Language Teaching or Language Learning?

The Reading–Writing Link

The more I become involved with teacher training, the more I am convinced that teachers have a store of knowledge developed over years of being successful teachers of reading. I believe this knowledge could be utilised to develop a New Zealand method of teaching children to write.

New Zealand educators such as Dame Marie Clay, Don Holdaway, Sylvia Ashton-Warner and Elwyn Richardson have contributed much to both teaching theory and practice. By blending their work with the best of overseas research, it would seem possible to construct a literacy learning model that would be superior to any system in the world.

Constructing meaning

It has often been said that 'The reader is the shadow of the writer and the writer is the shadow of the reader.' Another popular saying is 'We want our children to write like readers and read like writers.'

What do these sayings mean? Basically, they say that both processes are meaning-driven, both require the writer/reader to be an active participant, and both require active comprehension.

The reader has to be able to construct the meaning of the writer. The reader is saying, 'What does this writer mean? Do I understand the writer's intention?'

The writer is saying, 'Will my reader know what I mean? Have I explained it carefully and fully enough? What else do I need to say?'

Conveying meaning must be paramount in writing. After that, it is having the technical ability to put words down on paper. Finally, the abilities to cross over and read one's own writing in the guise of a reader is important. It is this last area, the comprehension of one's writing, that often gives children and teachers the most difficulty.

Early in 1994 I became engaged in researching children's beliefs and understandings about writing. One child remarked, 'I have to have the teacher read my writings because I read things that I think are there, but they aren't there at all.' Often the meaning is so obvious to the writer that the mind fills in all the details. The reader does not have the writer's background experiences to second-guess the text.

Revision – the writer's self-correction

What do readers do when they lose meaning? The answer is, of course, that they re-read (re-run) and self-correct. If teachers could observe students re-running and self-correcting during reading, they would be dismayed. Unfortunately, most teachers are unaware that these same strategies are equally important during writing. They therefore do not, first, teach these strategies, and second, reinforce these behaviours in the same way they would in reading.

Good writers re-run and self-correct when they lose meaning. This self-correction is called *revision*. If teachers cannot see children engaging in this process, they need to consider why children are not employing a self-correcting strategy. Some reasons for this neglect could be:

- the meaning is obvious to them.
- they are not considering the reader.
- they are not asking questions of their text.
- they don't know how to go about it.
- it has not been part of their instruction, therefore it has not become a matter of routine.
- some teachers encourage the use of revision; others are not interested.

Once again, teachers cannot expect children to use these strategies if they are never shown why or how. Children cannot use what they do not know or understand.

The NEMP provided a three-day test to see if children could apply revision strategies to their writing. *Day 1*: The topic was *My Place*. They were first motivated by being shown a whole variety of environments that might have meaning to the children. These included beaches, forests, city malls, apartment houses, bedrooms, suburban houses and sports fields. *Day 2*: The children were given time to write a draft about their favourite place. *Day 3*: The children were given time to revisit the piece, make additions, changes, deletions, proofread or even rewrite if they saw the need.

NEMP revision strategies data		% responses Year 4	Year 8
Extending (at end)	substantial	2	2
	slight	6	8
	none	92	90
Inserting (in middle)	substantial	0	2
	slight	6	14
	none	94	84
Reorganising	substantial	0	0
	slight	0	2
	none	100	98
Deleting	substantial	0	1
	slight	4	10
	none	96	89

The results reflect the fact that children do not see the need for or perhaps do not understand these processes and therefore do not see a reason for engaging in these behaviours. There is a full explanation about teaching these strategies in Chapter Five of this text.

A Broad-front Approach

Writing is not about having the ability to spell all the words, just as reading is not about being able to say all the words. The old 1961 syllabus had a statement that said, 'Spelling is a tool of written expression and not an end in itself.'

Donald Graves provides the following list in his text *Writers – Teachers and Children at Work* (Heinemann):

Spelling
Motor skill (Handwriting)
Surface conventions (Punctuation)
Information (Facts)
Revision (Clarification of Facts).

He believes that all five of these areas must be attended to from the first day at school. Sadly, he points out that most parents consider good writing to be spelling, handwriting and punctuation; meaning is not usually considered.

Many parents remember their own schooldays. They remember what teachers valued, and they know this was mainly the product.

A majority of parents believe good teachers demand accuracy of spelling, punctuation and neatness of work. Many of today's parents hated writing because they were poor spellers and not well coordinated.

I well remember my own school experiences. As an 11-year-old writer I learned how to write with my shoulders covering my ears. My teacher had the unfortunate habit of pointing to the error with the left hand, while flicking my ear with his right. I therefore wrote only the words I could spell and I kept my writing short. Less writing and fewer errors equals freedom from pain!

The reasons for writing

Most parents want their children to succeed at school and be better writers and spellers than they were. Unfortunately, many teachers, because of their own school experiences, make a habit of focusing on product when judging the quality of writing.

This is not to say that quality is unimportant. In fact, writing should be the goal of any school's writing programme. It is how the product is obtained that should be different to what has happened in years gone by.

The reason for teaching a process is to improve the product. A successful process should turn out a quality product. If the product is poor, the teacher needs to return to the processes. Is the problem with the pupil or is it with the teacher? In other words, is the teacher clear about what is being taught, and are learners clear about what they are expected to learn?

My 1994 research of 100 middle-school pupils showed that in only two of thirteen classes was there a clear understanding of the teacher's current learning agenda. In over 50 per cent of the classes, eight children interviewed gave eight different responses. Of the total response the highest number (18 per cent) gave the answer 'Don't know' or 'Nothing.' Out of the 100 children there were 45 different responses. Perhaps there are lessons to be drawn from such data.

Of course, the only way to get better writing is to ensure that children have real audiences and purposes. The NEMP interviews held with Year 4 and Year 8 children showed conclusively that many children identify the teacher as being their major audience. This was apparent in over 60 per cent of the responses.

If children are only writing for their teacher and classmates, there is a tendency not to include information that the reader already knows. This makes teaching *transactional* texts difficult because children: (a) have had common experiences or (b) believe the teacher already knows the information. This makes for purposeless writing. To quote an experience I had in Nelson:

Hood	Sometimes, I decide that I won't choose to communicate in writing. When might that occur?
	After some thought:
Boy	I wouldn't write if he was already here.
Hood	What do you mean by that?
Boy	If he is already here I'd just go over and tell him.
Hood	So when would you choose to write?
Boy	If he is not here.

So much in-class writing is just an academic exercise and has little purpose to the writer. Children do not want to put time into their products if there is no real purpose to the endeavour.

Reading and writing cues

Let us consider our New Zealand beliefs about the teaching of reading. Most teachers are now comfortable discussing the reading cueing systems. The beginning reader operates using experience, semantics and syntax. The beginning reader has little or no visual information to draw on. This information is developed as the child is introduced to reading and moves through an emergent reading programme. The emergent writer is in exactly the same position. Once again the visual cueing system is developed as the child moves through an emergent writing programme.

Mature readers and writers have a third cue. This is the visual system – the marks on the page. In both reading and writing this is the 'item' knowledge that enables writers and readers to encode/decode text. This is the graphophonic (the look and the sound) of language.

The Beginning Reader

Experience
↓   ↓
Semantics (Meaning)   Syntax (Language structure)

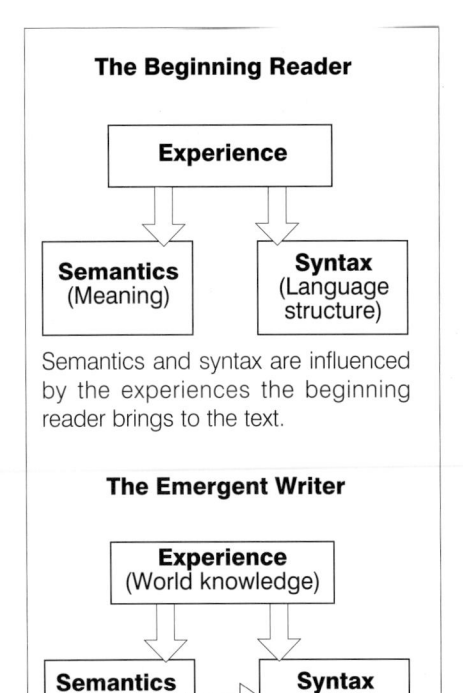

Semantics and syntax are influenced by the experiences the beginning reader brings to the text.

The Emergent Writer

Experience (World knowledge)
↓   ↓
Semantics (Convey meaning) → Syntax (Oral structure)

The experience of the emergent writer influences both semantics and syntax. Semantics also influences syntax.

Experience
Semantics
Syntax
Graphophonic
} **The reader and writer both use these cues**

The Importance of Experience

It is known that when children are unable to bring experience to text, reading becomes difficult. Readers have to draw heavily on visual information. They try to read the words. If a child does not have an extensive sight vocabulary, reading using this method becomes quite difficult. Often the reading becomes laboured as children try to decode word by word. These children often believe that reading is 'saying all the words'.

The writer must also have a background of experience. Donald Graves said, 'You can't write about nothing.' This was his reason for focusing on child topic choice and direct experience writing. He believed that young children learning how to put words down on paper were unlikely to find such teacher-imposed topics as 'My life as a ten-cent piece' – easy topics on which to write. How does a five or six-year-old know what it would be like to be a ten-cent piece?

Teachers of young children know that beginner writers do not often have problems thinking of writing topics. Their lives are full of rich and wonderful experiences, and they are egocentric enough to believe that everyone wants to know about them. Therefore they do not have any difficulty using semantic cues.

Unfortunately, many run into difficulty using syntactic cues. It seems that more and more children are arriving at school with immature patterns of oral language. My latest research seems to show that a large number of children are entering Invercargill schools at the lower end of the *Record of Oral Language* (Marie Clay and Assoc.). As I travel the country talking with teachers, this problem of an inadequate oral language base is a recurring theme.

The old saying that 'children who read more write better' is quite true. These children soak up 'book language'. This language is the language of description.

David Whitehead in his book *Catch Them Writing and Thinking* identifies three 'story' frameworks. In a simplistic form it breaks down like this:

Story 1   The ability to recall or retell using senses and memory (usually full of action verbs). *The Golden Gun* on pg. 37 is a good example.

Story 2   The ability to give reason (usually uses words like bust, because, so). *Bossy Boots* on pg. 23 is a good example.

Story 3   The ability to argue. The ability to describe. *Pirate Story on* pg. 84 is a good example.

▲ The writer must have a background of experience. As Donald Graves said, 'You can't write about nothing.'

> The NEMP descriptive piece *My Place* required children to use descriptive or *vivid* language. The results leave us with food for thought.
>
> | | | % response | |
> | --- | --- | --- | --- |
> | | | Year 4 | Year 8 |
> | **Vividness** | elements rich and vivid | 0 | 4 |
> | | good vivid description | 5 | 13 |
> | | some elements well described | 29 | 20 |
> | | none/very little vivid description | 66 | 43 |

This paucity of language must be addressed. Methods of developing this will be explored in Chapter 4.

If children have delayed oral language and limited visual knowledge, learning to read and write can be most difficult. New Zealand teachers have in the past engaged these children in initial reading by using a range of approaches:

- Reading to children
- Shared reading
- Shared writing (language experience).

The same approaches must be used in introducing children to writing. Teachers should monitor beginning writers against a similar list of behaviours as Margaret Mooney presented in *Developing Life-long Readers* (Department of Education, 1988).

When our team decided to develop a set of behaviours for *Dancing with the Pen,* we went back to *Developing Life-long Readers* and were amazed at how similar the behaviours were and how easy it was to translate writing behaviours from reading behaviours. Take, for instance, the following translations of early reading behaviours:[7]

1. Makes more accurate predictions. (Reading)
   to
   Spelling attempts closer to conventional forms. (Writing)
2. Reads on as well as re-runs to retain meaning. (Reading)
   to
   Re-reads and thinks on to attend to meaning. (Writing)
3. Chooses to read more frequently. (Reading)
   to
   Chooses to write more frequently. (Writing)
4. Confirms by checking known items. (Reading)
   to
   Starting to engage in proofreading. (Writing)

Writing Behaviours

While *Dancing with the Pen* gives an extensive list of writing behaviours, there are so many behaviours listed that most classroom teachers are not using them to monitor children. It is impossible to monitor each child against all of these behaviours. If teachers are

---

[7] See p. 11 of *Developing Life-long Readers* for a list of fluent reading behaviours.

going to use this list, they should select an aspect of the writing process and check children against that section of the list, e.g. p. 122 Topic and Ownership.[8]

The original idea of a list of writing behaviours was to enable teachers to take a sample of writing and match the behaviour to the sample, e.g. 'I am establishing principles of directionality.'

Some behaviours cannot be judged against a sample of work. These behaviours must be observed by the teachers during writing, e.g. 'I can read back my work,' or 'I can play my work orally.'

Summary of Key Points

The cues used in reading are the same as the cues used in writing.

Learning to read and learning to write are developmental processes.

A common set of behaviours can be used to monitor both processes.

Reading and writing progress are aided by sound oral language structures.

Good readers and good writers self-correct when meaning is lost.

The teaching approaches in both reading and writing are basically the same.

---

[8] See Appendix 1, p. 121 of *Dancing with the Pen*, Learning Media, Wellington, 1991.

2

In this chapter

- The influence of parents on beginning writers
- Observing the new entrant
- Writing programmes for juniors
- The five specifics of writing
- 'Talk written down'
- Activities that help and hinder learning
- Revision
- The role of the teacher

Emerging As a Writer

Marie Clay, speaking about reading, remarked, 'There is no substitute for good first teaching.' This is also true of emergent writing programmes.

During the first weeks of instruction, children will gain either a positive or negative image of themselves as writers. The classroom programme dictates whether they become risk-takers or dependent learners. Sadly for some, this mindset has already been cast before they reach the classroom.

The Influence of Parents on Beginning Writers

Parents are well-meaning people, and many believe they are expert in matters educational. After all, didn't they attend school? They know how they were taught and, like many teachers, often teach in the same way. For many, beginning writing instruction means caption copying.

Today's world has placed more stresses and strains on parents than ever before. Most know that finding employment is difficult. Wanting the best for one's child is quite natural. It is also natural that parents try to ensure their children make the best possible transition from home to school. Some parents have already begun to teach their children to read and write. For many, this is an advantage; for a few it is a handicap.

Children as copiers rather than writers

The problem is not that children have had this instruction, rather that the methods used are at odds with current educational theory. Often parents give children captions to copy. They think back to what happened when they went to school. Most children quickly take to this copying task. Unfortunately, the hidden message is that the parent can write, the child can copy. Many new entrants believe they cannot write, but these children are often excellent copiers.

More often than not these children are not risk-takers. They know there is a correct way to write. They know about words, and how they are used to construct messages. They also have acquired advanced motor skills. They know that when learning one is either correct or wrong. Many have been conditioned into thinking that making mistakes is just 'not nice'. Often these children are very hard to work with. Although they have had a wide range of literacy experiences, there is an expectation that adults will supply their written text and they will copy.

So What Can Parents Do?

There are some key things that parents should be encouraged to do to prepare their child for school. These include:
- Writing in front of the child. The child needs to see print modelled.
- Encourage them to experiment with pen and paper. Allow the child to write before any captioning activity.
- Teach the child to recognise the alphabet.
- If teaching them to print letters, try for correct directionality.
- Give them the attitude that writing is fun.

Observing the New Entrant

It is important to develop positive attitudes in children to writing. Teachers should therefore begin by collecting as much data as possible on the new entrant. The easiest way to do this is to supply pencil and paper and ask the child to draw a picture.

1. Observe:
- How does the child hold the pencil? (Pencil grip? Like a dagger? Like a sword?)
- How does the child view the world? (People? Objects? Scribble?)
- Observe attempts at drawing people. (All head; head, arms, legs attached or floating?)
- Do the drawings show head and body? Are these connected? Does the child put in eyes, mouth, teeth?
- Does the child draw legs, feet, great big fingers?
- Do the drawings sit on a base line?
- Does the child include the sun, clouds, rainbows, trees, leaves, houses, pets?
- How does the child show relative size between dad, mum and children?
- Can the child draw at all or does he or she just scribble?

This sort of data should provide the teacher with some idea of the child's previous pencil and paper experiences.

2. Talk to the child. Observe:
- Willingness to discuss a picture.
- Ability to converse in sentences.
- Does art work have a central theme, or show a range of unrelated objects?
- Check oral language against *Record of Oral Language* (Marie Clay & Assoc.)
- Is oral language adequate, superior or delayed?
- How will this influence what you teach?

3. Ask the child to write. Observe:
Does the writer:
- Write his or her name?
- Write words?

Hinsan
Friday 7 October
My car has a spare wheel at the back. Only two persons can sit in the car. The spare wheel is useful. If one of the wheels has a puncture I can swap it around.

Imagine if we had a bull and I had a red tulip and the bull came charging at me. I would do a flip onto it. It would try to kick me off but I am too smart.

[9] *Language experience* is the development of reading materials based on the child's own language.

- Write letters upper case? Lower case?
- String letters together across the page?
- Understand about gaps between words?
- Attempt any letter/sound links? (e.g. The child who wrote wdww – One day we went.)
- Read back the writing?
- Ask you to read it?
- Do nothing?

4. Find out:
- What is the child's knowledge of the alphabet?

Teachers cannot develop programmes for learners until they know what learners can do for themselves. For some children there may be a need to engage in shared writing so that they see how text is written down. For others it may be desirable to expose them to some key vocabulary so that they can start to attempt sentence construction.

Some children may need to spend further time drawing. The teacher's role will be to engage the child in conversation, broadening and extending oral language. More able students will need to establish the concept of word, spaces between words, and a method of attempting to spell unknown words. Often with this latter group, what is needed is to encourage the child to take a risk with spelling. The teacher should praise the attempt rather than the accurately spelled word.

Writing Programmes for Juniors

Writing time for juniors is a time of experimentation. Children try out their beliefs and confirm or reject as they match up their efforts with teacher demonstrations. As with learning to talk, learning occurs when the child perceives a mismatch. In writing they discover a mismatch between how they write and how the teacher writes.

In *Dancing with the Pen* I told the story of a child who explained that her writing and the teacher's written model were the same – 'the teacher copied off me.' She did not learn from the situation because she did not have the linguistic development to perceive the mismatch. Developmentally, she had not discovered anything about words, spaces and their relationship to message.

Teaching juniors is about giving the learner opportunity to observe and make connections, but the writing time is only a minor part of the total language programme. These children must be exposed to print through:
- shared writing
- helping them read enlarged-text books
- engaging in share readings of books during instructional reading
- exploring letters and words during reading and language
- helping teachers write labels for displays
- learning the alphabet
- reading wall stories.[9]

The thirty-minute writing time, or the time the child chooses to write, is the time when this learning is put to use.

Time to write
There is no one way to organise a time for writing. While it is important that these children write daily, the classroom management strategies are very much open to individual interpretation.
- Some teachers let the children pick when and for how long they write. Books are put into an *I have written today* box. After the mid-morning break the teacher reminds those who have not written that they now have to write. Teachers know who they want to see and make sure they get next to these individuals during the morning.
- Some teachers like all their children writing at the same time. Teachers move around the groups helping children.
- Some call in groups of children in much the same way as they would call in reading groups, so they get next to these individuals during the morning.
- Teachers working in two-person teams may have one teacher who works with children preparing work for publication, while the second teacher takes on a roving role.

▲ Penny, a five-year-old, tries writing on her first day at school.

The Five Specifics of Writing
In his book *Writers – Teachers and Children at Work* (Heinemann) Donald Graves mentions five specifics of writing that need to be attended to at every level of education. They are spelling, motor skills, surface features, information and topic. Let us consider the importance of these in teaching emergent writing.

Spelling
It is important that children develop a systematic method of attempting unknown words. Although they might not go into the senior school as correct spellers, they should have a large bank of known high-frequency words. They should also be able to make close visual approximations of other words using sound sequencing techniques.

Donald Graves in his new book *A Fresh Look at Writing* mentions the fact that he used to believe that children could get under way with writing if they knew a few sounds. Now he believes that there is a core of known words that beginning writers must learn to write automatically. He lists the following:

I *	is *	am	come	see	the *
we	at	on	look	this	a *
in *	to *	like	me	my	and *
here	up	go	it *	you *	of *
that *					

He states that the * words comprise 25 per cent of all written language. Graves also points out that these words are almost identical to the beginning reading sight list of Dame Marie Clay.

Sound sequencing means being able to hear the sounds within words and being able to map these. Dr Richard Gentry, a world authority in spelling research, says that although people do not learn to spell using applied phonics, they manage to get close enough visually to use dictionaries and other spelling resources to check their approximations. If this self-correction does not occur then the children do not quickly move to becoming correct spellers.[10]

Children must be taught how to say the word slowly and to listen to their own voices. They should do this several times, putting the sounds down in order as they write. It is not enough to put down just the first and last letter. This can lead to lazy spelling as the child leaves the rest to the teacher. They must record all they can hear.

My 1994 research showed that 29 per cent of eight-to-ten-year-old children interviewed used a *sound it out* strategy, while 28 per cent used a *sound it, underline, check in dictionary later* strategy. I believe that this identification and checking approach is the one that must be taught. When children are close to visually correct they must be eased into this self-correction. The NEMP results stress how important it is that schools develop a common method of error identification. The time to identify probable error is at the time of writing, not going back to hunt for errors after the writing is complete.

The ability to write quickly and efficiently enables the writer to get thoughts down on paper. Testing writing out on a piece of paper and confirming with the teacher ('she will write it for me') may produce a greater number of accurate spellings but slows down the flow of writing. It also puts the responsibility for spelling back on the teacher. Children do not mind teachers doing their thinking for them. As children generate a few words, teachers become more and more involved in helping children with spelling.

Observation of new-entrant children during the first half of 1994 showed clearly that those who had superior alphabet knowledge moved quickly into writing and made logical attempts at spelling. Children who were bright but had little alphabet knowledge soon closed this gap. Average-to-less-able children found this lack of letter knowledge a handicap. It would seem that boosting alphabet knowledge by identifying what letters are known and then gradually learning the other letters aids writing development.

In working with teachers during the Ministry of Education 1991 writing contract, I heard junior school teachers regularly complain that all their conferences with children were about spelling. In fact, all these conferences were about meaning, as you cannot have meaning until you have words on the page.

Although this process of teaching children to sound sequence spelling may seem like a daily grind, there are no shortcuts. Some children have naturally strong visual retention systems and quickly make excellent approximations. Others may take a year to develop this ability, some two years, while some may always struggle with spelling. Teachers should set themselves realistic learning objectives for each learner. Unfortunately, there are no easy answers, just hard work.

So, how important is it that the beginning writer can spell? A good written sight vocabulary is just as important to being able to write as an

---

[10] A *correct speller* uses correct forms, but may be thwarted by irregularities in the English language.

internalised sight vocabulary is to reading. The ability to write a number of high-frequency words enables the child to maintain meaning and give attention to spelling the interest words. Readers, especially teachers, are then able to read what is written and guide the learners in their approximations. When approximations are occurring more often than one word in five, reading becomes very difficult.

I have yet to see a child who is strong in the use of *'invented spelling'* who invents everything. These children have a large range of known words. They only have to approximate the high interest words, and these are usually already close to being accurate. The logic is that if you can't spell, you can't write. Spelling should not be neglected. Chapter 6 deals with this subject more fully.

To this end I would supply a range of high-frequency words for the writer. These may be provided via wall alphabet lists or may be written on large flashcards. These cards are then thrown out on the floor and the children are encouraged to look for the words they need. Another method is to make *'word blocks'*. These can be constructed by taping two wine casks together, covering them with cartridge paper, and writing four of the above high-frequency words on each face of the cube. These can be put in the middle of each group table. If children copy them down often enough, they will soon commit them to memory. Once again, learning to read and learning to write are tightly locked together. If the child can't recognise the word, the child can't find the word. Every time the children locate, copy and read, their chances of remembering these words are increased.

Simple one-word-per-page dictionaries are also useful. These books are useful for developing proper nouns. They can be clearly illustrated and are very useful to young writers. At the same time I would point out that beginner dictionaries with numerous words on each page, all starting with the same letter, are more likely to confuse than help.

The teacher's role is to remind children where certain words may be found. The philosophy is self-help, not teacher supply.

Motor skill

The ability to produce a reasonable standard of handwriting is a great aid to a writer. It makes the reader's task easier too. If children can make letters without worrying about where to start, they will be able to give greater attention to spelling and message.

During our 1994 observations of new entrant writers, it was amazing to note that most of these beginning writers continually re-read their writing before writing the next word. Every time a new word was added the writer had to return to the start of the piece and recall the memory. It seems that writing the latest word destroyed their memory for how the piece was developing. Writing words seems quite demanding, both physically and mentally, for these children. If children can print quickly and neatly, spelling and message seem to flow from the writer's pen.

It is important that children learn the correct starting points and finishing points for each letter. When they have to start linking letters, they need to finish in the correct place. There should be no need for

---

ATEFN AND UC KLIN

Yesdaday atefn and un Klin went on a plane the plane is a big plane. We ddt go and see atefn and unc Klin go on the plane ma and pa tk tm to th erupt. etc.

▲ Dale, a six-year-old, wrote this story. The story title reads 'Auntie Fran and Uncle Colin'.

BOSSY BOOTS

I name Michelle B.B. because she pulled me out of my bed. She through an ice cream at me but it went in mum's face. But I went outside because I did not want to see Michelle get smacked.

▲ Andrea, also a six-year-old, wrote this story. Note the spelling – through/threw.

these children to have to break bad habits. Regular instruction in handwriting would seem to be a necessary part of classroom programmes.

Having a sound pencil grip is also important. Writers who write for long periods of time develop muscular stress and handwriting suffers. A comfortable, correct grip reduces this fatigue.

Surface features

This term refers to basic print conventions: knowing about sentences, full stops, capitals or proper names, question marks, exclamation marks and speech marks. The objective should be to make children aware of how and when these are used. Most will have these understandings in place by the end of their third year at school. A few will be using more complex methods of punctuation; a few will still struggle with simple sentences.

It is important that teachers write in front of their children, showing how they punctuate their work. It is equally important to show children how adults think.

Teacher   I want to write, 'I am going to town after school to do my shopping.' That is my first sentence. I will start with a capital letter 'I'. Now, who remembers what I was going to say? Marie?

Marie   You were going to write, 'I am going to town today to do my shopping.'

The teacher then works on through the sentence, re-running often to keep track of the message.

Teacher   Now I have finished my sentence I need to put in a full stop. What will I write next? What will my readers want to know? What do you think I need to say? Karl?

Karl   What did you buy?

Teacher   'I bought my groceries at the supermarket.' This will be my next sentence.

I am convinced that many children are unaware that writers think in sentences. They think what they are going to write, put it down, place the full stop, think out the next sentence.

Discussing punctuation with a nine-year-old, I was told that her teacher always told the class, 'Don't forget when you have finished writing, go through and put in your full stops.' How often have I said this to children? If children do not have the opportunity to observe how adults write and understand how adults think, this reasoning is quite understandable. This child was convinced that you write first and punctuate second. Where children are exposed to daily newsboard programmes, it is not uncommon to find five-year-old children who use many of these punctuation devices accurately. They see their teachers using different methods of punctuation and they try these out during their own writing.[11]

Information

Most parents would say that good writing is neat, correctly spelled, and properly punctuated. Often the message is something that is not considered. As teachers we must always be conscious that of the five

[11] 'Newsboard' involves recording oral news in writing. This approach uses word finding, punctuating, alternative language, word-building, etc. The learner decides what will be learned. No short-term mastery goals are expected. A video on 'Newsboard' is currently being produced by the A.V. Department, Dunedin College of Education, Private Bag, Dunedin. Available 1998.

elements listed, information and revision of meaning must not be neglected. Revision at this stage is adding to the message.

I got some new shoes.
Becomes:
I got some new shoes. They are black.

Topic and the five-year-old

New-entrant children do not have problems with finding topics. During my 1994 research I did not see one five-year-old struggle for a topic. Most wrote a new piece every day and nearly all were either about 'I' or 'we'. The egocentric nature of the five-year-old makes finding topics easy.

Many rehearse their topics before they get to school. They discuss their topics over breakfast, think them over as they walk to school, and remember interesting experiences from the day before.

Some do not know what they are going to write until after they do their drawings. Sometimes these drawings develop this way:
1. Put in sun, clouds, rainbows.
2. Put in house, tree, the writer.
3. Put in another agent – dog, cat, parent, brother, sister, friend, etc.
4. Decide on what is happening.

It is not uncommon for young children to draw clouds (scribble to us) the sun, rainbow, rain and themselves. Their pictures do not have any action as such. Similarly, children in their writing do not think in sentences or describe action. Children who have not had many experiences with text go through a discovery phase as they try to work out what writing is and what they have to say.

Oral language is the key to writing. Our 1994 research showed a very high correlation between oral language ability and the learner's growth as a writer. One might be tempted to ask, if you cannot think in sentences, or speak in sentences or how do you write in sentences?

A survey taken in Invercargill city schools of February/March new entrant children points to 30 per cent of these children experiencing some degree of language delay. In one area of the city this percentage went up to 46 per cent. This makes early literacy teaching difficult, and I believe this trend could well be reflected in many areas of New Zealand, if not internationally.

Donald Graves said, 'Writing flows on a sea of speech.' If a child's sea is a puddle, the child is severely disadvantaged. I must emphasise the importance of speaking prior to writing. All children need opportunity to generate their language, but for children who have inadequate oral language, oral language modelling and speaking must come before writing.

'Talk Written Down'

A common statement often made about writing is that writing is 'talk written down'. We now know this is not true.

Recent work undertaken in trying to make sense of the oral language strand of the national curriculum has focused teachers' attention on *conversational* oral language and how it is different to *written* oral language. Most five-year-old children are sound users of conversational oral language. They manage to make their point of view known to all their friends in the playground, but do not bring to the classroom the type of patterning that teachers expect and demand.

The way children speak
Let us consider what happens when children engage in conversations:
- it is usually one-on-one topics.
- the topic is clear to both participants.
- often the object being discussed is on hand.
- if meaning is not clear you can question.
- the speaker only gives enough information to answer the question.
- 'ahs' and 'umms' are common.
- speakers often repeat themselves or rephrase (especially if body language from the listener tells them they don't understand).
- words that have no meaning – such as 'well' – are often used.

Grice (1975) developed a set of rules that seem to fit this view of communication:
1. Quantity: Don't provide more information than the exchange requires.
2. Quality: Try to say what is true.
3. Manner: Be clear.
4. Avoid ambiguity.
5. Avoid obscurity.
6. Be brief.
7. Be orderly.

Take this example:
 'What did you get at the shop?'
 'Shoes.'
 'What colour were they?'
 'Black.'
 'Are you wearing them?'
 'Yes.'
 'Who went shopping with you?'
 'My big brother and sister.'
 'Was it fun?'
 'No.'
 'Why not?'
 'I don't like the bus.'

The importance of drawing
Drawing is an important link between being able to think and construct language in sentences. The teacher can learn a lot from the responses to questions. Take this example: The child has drawn a picture of a boat.
Teacher   Tell me about your picture.
Child   It's a boat.
Compare it with this:

Teacher   Tell me about your picture.
Child   The boat is sailing on the sea.

The second child knows that oral language has to be expressed in a different way if it is going to be written down. The child understands the difference between the written and spoken form. This understanding of structure relates back to the child's early literacy experiences and gives the teacher excellent information about the likely starting point for instruction.

This is why drawing is so important. If there is a drawing on the page, there is something to talk about. If the page is blank, how does one draw out language from the child?

Teacher arriving at Bryan's desk:
Teacher   What are you drawing about today, Bryan?
Bryan   A fish.
Teacher   Where is the fish, Bryan?
Bryan   Uncle's boat.
Teacher   So, what are you going to write?
Bryan   Uncle caught fish.
Teacher   You are going to say, 'My uncle caught a fish.' What are you going to say?
Bryan   My uncle caught fish.

It is going to take time and patience to increase Bryan's oral ability, but that is the teaching challenge.

Verbalising writing

More able language users also need opportunities to verbalise their writing. A routine where children discuss their picture with their neighbour and say what they are going to write seems to help children organise their thinking:

Lynette   This is my tree and I am in the trees looking at the bird. See the big blackbird flying? 'I am in the tree looking at the nest.' What are you going to write today?
Thomas   This is our car and I am holding the wheel. This is Tony working on the car. I'm writing, 'I helped Tony fix the car.'

Sharing the message is a skill that will be required in later schooling when children are asked to engage in partner conferencing.

Another excellent routine is to have children read their completed text to their neighbour. Although I have sometimes observed both children reading at the same time, the fact that they have an audience for their writing seems to give the children a sense of purpose.

My 1994 research gave me ample opportunity to observe emergent writers. I have seven hours of video showing one group of children. These videos were taken as the children engaged in independent writing and follow progress from week three to week thirteen of their first term at school.

▲ Drawing is an important link between being able to think and construct language in sentences. Each of these pieces of work has been done by six-year-olds. The upper story records news that might have been discussed in class. The lower page is from Nicole's book, *The Funeral*.

It was interesting to observe the major role their drawings played in helping them formulate their ideas. Most talked as they drew and many turned over various sentence patterns during drawing:

Child A   I am in the tree
Child B   This is me. I am in the house.
Child C   This is me. I am playing.

'This is me' was commonly used as a starting point. It gave the children a sense of identity and reinforced the purpose of writing to tell about 'me'!

Children were often observed going back to the beginning of their books and reading everything that had been written. Often others would stop and listen. Here is one recorded incident:

Child A   This is me at school.
                I am helping mum.
                This is me playing.
                This is me walking to school.
                This is me in the tree.
Child B   I've got that one too. (Finds page.) 'This is me in the tree.'
Child C   Hey – I've got that one as well. (Finds page.) 'This is me up the tree.'

Most of these children quickly moved through to writing some words. Only one of the five was still stringing letters together by the eleventh week.

There was general discussion about words: how they were spelled, how they started, where they could be found. Much time was spent in comparing words on cards, in alphabet books, in other books and from one child's book to another. The children noted how they were spelled, picking out words that were spelled the same. It was interesting to note how they attached new knowledge to old.

Other parts of the writing process were also discussed: pages used, pages still to come, how many lines on a page. Who used what colour, and why? Did plane start with a 'p'? Was it the black word or was it in the blue words above? (The black word being the noun and the blue words a sentence using the noun.) Has anyone else got a plane? The debate about church: did it start with a 't' or a 'c'? We found that, left to their own devices, children did teach each other.

When the teacher arrived at the group, all talk ceased. They were now too interested in what the teacher was showing one of their group. This supports the theory that teachers who spend quality time with one child in a group are in fact teaching everyone.

Activities that Help and Hinder Learning

These things seemed to help children learn:
- constant re-running of their writing attempts.
- talking about their drawings.
- asking others for help.
- comparing their writing.

- discussing words and how they are spelled.
- using one picture, one word, one page word resources.
- making comparisons between pieces of writing, i.e. reading like pieces.
- discussing what page to write on and where to write.
- drawing others' attention to missing letters in words.
- having alphabet cards, pictures and word.
- having cards with a few high-frequency words (Leaves on a tree. Petals on a flower.).
- reading their writing to others.
- talking aloud as they write.

These things seemed to hinder their learning:
- alphabetical dictionaries. On a number of occasions children spent between ten and fifteen minutes hunting for words they could not read. On several occasions the words were not present.
- trying to be accurate at all times. They used a range of resources but lacked the ability to approximate spelling.

It was impressive watching these children solve problems. It was obvious that there was more than one teacher in this classroom. They seemed to learn as much from each other as from the teacher. It shows that one cannot control what, how or when children learn.

The difference is, of course that teachers can evaluate the child's work and should be able to identify learning goals. Teachers are managers of learning experiences; this should then enable the child to do the learning. The old saying, 'Language is caught, not taught', took on new meaning watching these children.

Revision

As already mentioned, revision at this level is adding to the text. Teachers usually introduce this by asking individual children questions about their writing. It is usually only

This shows a piece of work developed from draft to final form. ▼

Tomorrow we are going to Guy Fawkes with my uncle and mum and my sister to look at it. Then we go home to bed to wake up and have a good rest and be a good boy.

by Thomas

introduced when children are able to comfortably construct a single sentence, and the teacher is trying to get the child to extend the message.

This is most useful if a child becomes locked into a particular sentence pattern. It is not uncommon for some children to learn how to write a sentence such as: 'I am at the park.' They then use it every day for several weeks.

The reason for this is security. When children think they have mastered something, there is a need to consolidate this learning. Some children lack the confidence to move outside the known sentence. It is then that the teacher asks questions to try to break this comfortable pattern:

Teacher   What did you do at the park?
Terry   I played on the swings.
Teacher   Do you think the other children would want to know what you did?

Now, this might pose a problem. If Terry has never read his writing to the class and they have never asked any questions, he will not worry one way or another. If his writing has been questioned in the past, there is usually reason to add to the text – the demands of an audience!

Terry   Yes.
Teacher   How will you write 'I'?
            How will you write 'played'?

The teaching task now becomes one of helping the child revise the original message to put words down on paper. If the child does not believe the children want to be informed, the teacher leaves it at that – *but* makes sure that the child is up front reading the piece and making sure that lots of questions follow.

Here is an example of a Year Five girl who was very capable at undertaking her own revisions:

Child   (Thinking as she reviews her writing.) We went down to Henderson's Bush. They will say, 'Why call it Henderson's Bush?' The child 'arrows in' to the text and adds '… and is named after the Henderson family who own the farm.'

This type of self-dialogue is what we want our writers to be able to achieve. Much depends on the child being exposed to thousands of demonstrations of questions and responses.

During the 1991 Ministry of Education Writing Contract some teachers observed that there were a large number of five-year-old children who could not ask questions. These were, significantly, the same children who were experiencing learning difficulties.

All child development textbooks say that three- and four-year-old children question, some continually. Sadly, some children have lost this ability prior to entering school. Is it because adults do not give them answers? Are they told, 'Be quiet; don't talk such nonsense'? I am sure that these types of responses influence new-entrant child behaviour.

To observe parents as teachers, one only has to stand beside the deep freeze at any supermarket during school holidays. It is interesting to watch parents react to their children. Some speak, answer questions, extend concepts, encourage dialogue. Others shout, hit, pull, curse, drag. Is it any wonder some children do not speak readily to adults and do not question in class? This latter group of children should give all teachers great concern.

A method of teaching children to ask questions has already been outlined in this book. Needless to say, it is the task of the new entrant teacher to reawaken this ability if somewhere along the line the child has given up on being a questioner.

Junior Class Children and the Curriculum

I mentioned earlier the fact that some schools are trying to force young children to write *expressively*, *poetically* and *transactionally*, and that they are often trying to teach children genres that they are not developmentally ready for.

Donald Graves states in his new text, *A Fresh Look at Writing*, that he would not consider formal instruction of writing with Grade One children. He states that first they need to learn about writing.

I would point out that the child can't write *expressively, poetically* or *transactionally* until they can write. They can't write until they can speak, and they can't write until they have developed some control over spelling and the physical mechanics of writing. I feel teachers are losing sight of their role. The aim of the junior school is to teach them to write, not to teach genre.

I believe that if teachers are pedantic about the need to collect such samples, any piece of junior school writing could be placed within a sub-strand.

Here is the car (Transactional – it gives information)
Yesterday I went to grandma's (Start of a recount)
The dog chased the rabbit (Poetic)
Today I am going to David's (Expressive).

But who cares? Let's worry about getting children to the stage where they can put their thoughts fluently on paper before getting hung up on the technicalities of genre.

The Role of the Teacher

So how should the teacher of new-entrant children engage their class in writing? 'What do I do?' is probably the most asked question I am faced with during teacher workshops.

First, the teacher must be seen to be a writer. Sound, regular demonstrations of how adults think, write and question are essential. The teacher must show not only the composing process, but all the other problem-solving strategies mature writers have at their disposal.

The teacher should show that even for adults spelling is at times a problem. Adult writers have strategies to overcome these problems; it is the application of these strategies that children need to be able to

Some Key Conclusions

Find out what the child can do – skills, beliefs, language.

Oral language is a major factor in writing.

Drawings are a window to the mind.

Children should be expected to draw and write from their first day at school.

Alphabet knowledge is a major aid to writing.

Children must be encouraged to be risk-takers. They must be given a method to attack unknown words.

Writers need audiences. Children should obtain a variety of responses to their writing.

Questioning is an important skill. Teachers might have to reawaken this ability in some learners.

Quality time with a few is better than spreading the time across many.

Young children are problem-solvers. A lot of their learning comes from other children.

There is no one way to organise for writing.

Children need to meet the written word in variety of contexts.

observe. I don't mean teachers should make mistakes for the sake of making mistakes. I believe that teachers should be giving children realistic demonstrations of self-doubt, and showing how these doubts are overcome. I often see young – and sometimes the not-so-young – teachers trying to bluff their way through these difficulties. What does it prove? Why can't adults admit to their failings when they are unsure or just do not know the answers?

Second, the teacher must provide an environment where children are 'doomed to succeed'. If children think writing is difficult, they will always be reluctant writers. Writing time at this level must be a time to experiment, enjoy, and above all succeed. It is not a time for intensive teaching. If the child shares an environment where text is being explored in a variety of contexts, I am sure there will develop a sound understanding of the written word. This is what a whole-language classroom delivers to the learner: an environment where text and language are investigated in context, and where children are trusted to learn.

In my opinion, of all the areas within the school system, the teacher of new-entrant children probably carries the greatest responsibility. The child's path through school may well be determined by the experiences shared during these first months of instruction.

Why the Fuss About Genre?

In this chapter

- The issues
- Middle-school programmes
- Writing across the curriculum
- Using the curriculum
- Retaining the best aspects of process writing
- A planned method of genre development
- A plan of work for Years Four to Six
- School review: questions to ask

During the second half of the 1980s, while New Zealand teachers were still arguing the merits of process writing, Australian teachers were also engaged in debate. The Australian debate was not centred on process vs product; rather it was based on the opposing philosophies of free choice (process writing) vs directed teaching (genre). This Australian debate was one of the reasons why an emphasis was placed on cross-curriculum writing in *Dancing with the Pen* (Learning Media, 1991).

The Australian debate focused on two groups of educationalists who held opposing points of view. On one hand the process writing camp held a philosophy based on the concept of child ownership. These educators believed that purpose would dictate when children learned about formal genres of writing. On the other hand, the genre supporters believed that teachers should plan to teach children to write in many different genres and that this should not be left to chance.

Our aim as authors of *Dancing with the Pen* was to keep the best of both philosophies by teaching both processes and genres. This chapter will discuss how we arrived at this decision and will endeavour to give some direction as to how this balance can be achieved.

The Issues

By 1987 it became obvious to those of us working in teacher education that something had to be done about classroom programmes. There was an awareness that the Australians were debating the genre question, while the 1984 IEA survey also had delivered some timely words of warning. This survey had discovered that Year Eleven students, while sound at writing letters and narratives, were generally uncomfortable at handling more formal writing genres.

Pupils performed better on the letter-writing tasks and the narrative. Students wrote best when the content and register were familiar. They were less experienced in using the formal register (IEA Report, 1984).

Donald Graves (1982) had also recounted that many first-year American college students did not have basic skills in writing non-fiction. They did not know how to select research studies, develop a point of view, use reference materials, take notes or explain a view 'honestly and with a sense of voice'.

He discovered that many bright pupils had drifted through the school system simply by being able to reproduce given information. This ability to second-guess the teacher had seen them through senior high and into college. Suddenly they found the ground rules were quite different. Now the professors turned the tasks back on the pupils.

They had to be able to pick their topic, pick a stance, research and write in order to convince the professors of their knowledge.

Having spent most of his time teaching at a tertiary level Graves remarked, 'Sadly many did not have the skills, abilities, and adaptability to survive.' He was able to observe that students needed to quickly learn around 'real' writing. Graves contended that 'the writer, not the teacher, now becomes the authority'. Graves wondered why they had to wait so long to learn such an important lesson.

During the years 1985–88 our writing team spent time individually researching children's writing. I worked extensively with younger writers, and was surprised to see the emergence of a clear pattern of genre development. My observation suggested that the first three years of schooling produced a natural development of several writing genres. This development occurred without any form of planned teacher intervention.

A three-year development
- Write labels to go with pictures.
- Write observations about their world and comment on them.
- Recount personal experiences.
- Write letters to friends and family.
- Retell known stories.

This seemingly natural development seems to grow out of children's increasing language maturity and the literacy-based programmes common to junior school classrooms.

```
Really!  These Americans.  So excitable!  Not like us British.
I stopped and slipped slightly and I could hear them all draw in
their breath in horror.  I made my way slowly down.  As I reached
the bottom a hundred hands - or so it seemed - reached out to
help me down.
```

▲ A page from Sarah's book *Lost in a Skyscraper*. Sarah was a Year Eight student when she wrote this story.

Many teachers show a reluctance to encourage their children to write subject-based non-fiction, yet young writers' earliest writing attempts are non-fiction. Writing fiction is something that occurs later in the child's writing development.

Children first draw pictures and are usually invited by their teachers to write. The translations of these attempts usually follow a stylised pattern. This form of writing is known as *labelling:*
This is my... Here is my... We are... I am...

Teachers next encourage children to make observations and comments through questioning the writer:

Child	Here is my dog.
Teacher	What is your dog doing?
Child	He is sleeping in the sun.
Teacher	How would you write that? Can you write 'he'?

So the story now reads:
Here is my dog. He is sleeping in the sun.

The above shows two direct observations made from the picture of the dog. Another statement, this time a comment, could be elicited from the child.

Teacher	Why do you think he is sleeping?
Child	Because he is tired.

The story might now read:
Here is my dog. He is sleeping. I think he is tired.

The writer now has two observations and one comment.

It would seem that the skills of making observations of the world and developing reasoned comment are prerequisites for scientific writing. When one considers that writing in science requires the writer to observe and make comments about a variety of processes, this early 'observation and comment' writing seems to be an important step in developing these abilities.

Another interesting observation I would make about this type of writing is that most children tend to tack the comment on the end. How many teachers recognise the final statement 'It was cool fun'?

I have observed many quite gifted young writers, and a common factor is their ability to mist the comments among the observations. They often use the words 'because' or 'so that'. I believe these examples of writing can be used to identify gifted writers at an early stage of their development. Take these two examples:

I went to Tom's house. We played in the sandpit with his trucks. My mother picked me up at five o'clock. It was cool fun.

I went to Tom's house because my mother was out shopping. We played in the sandpit with his trucks so his mother could get on with her work. My mother picked me up at five o'clock. It was cool fun.

The use of comment in the second piece is quite marked.

> **THE RED TULIP AND THE BULL**
>
> On the bus was fun because we got to go up to Makarewa. I saw the tulip farms, there were all sorts of tulips. I brought a red one to school. Imagine if we had a bull and I had a red tulip and the bull came charging at me. I would do a flip onto it. It would try to kick me off but I am too smart. Imagine if I truly done that. It would be dangerous.
>
> Jason (Age 6.10 years)

▲ This short story purposely mixes recount and narrative.

> Dear Adam
> Myn cat is ding nte thigs. I am going in the cr to scl
> From Matthew
>
> Matthew (Age 5.3 years)

▲ A young writer's attempt at letter-writing.

> **SNOOPY**
>
> One day Mum, Dad and I went to the Dawson's. We went on Saturday night. Dad and Mr Dawson went on Saturday night. Dad and Mr Dawson went to the hotel and Mum and Mrs Dawson got tea. Their cat had kittens. when they came home I asked Mr Dawson if I could have a kitten. 'Only if your dad lets you' he said. So I asked dad. 'When the kittens are older we might' he said.
>
> Sonia (Age 8 years)

▲ A personal recount.

Recount

As children develop their ability to use inventive spelling systems, the number of observations and comments increase. Children also now move towards recounting personal experiences.

To quote Graves again, 'Recounting in order with an interpretation of events is the underpinning of all human thought.'

Most junior class children will say that this is good writing. They will tell you it is their best story 'because it is long'. For some this is their first true success as a writer. They believe they have arrived. Teachers should not be too critical of these first rambling attempts, but celebrate with the child their growing skills.

Often the recount develops into the child's first efforts at writing fiction. Perhaps they cannot remember all of the experience or perhaps they stretch the truth a little to make the story more interesting. To quote Graves (1988), 'Some children ... regularly narrate fiction when recounting real events, enjoying the feel of an outcome they wish had happened.' In point of fact, they tell lies.

An interesting aside is that when this happens in writing the teacher praises the child's imagination. If, however, the child was to tell this story orally, the child would probably be given some strange looks and some may even mention his 'stretching of the truth'. It just shows how much reliance people put on the spoken word.

Narrative

Sometimes children mix recount and narrative on purpose, as in the story of *The Red Tulip and the Bull*. A more common stepping out into narrative occurs with the retelling of a known story. For many this is the first step outside of self. Best friends become the main characters, and generally the writer becomes the storyteller rather than the hero.

Letters

Children also write letters. Teachers introduce children to letter-writing early in their schooling as there are always field-trips that offer real purposes and audiences.

When children have a known audience, purpose and adequate opportunities to write, letter-writing can be an excellent vehicle for encouraging reluctant writers. There must, however, be an element of choice, as many children have had their interest in writing letters destroyed by being forced to do them.

Middle-School Programmes

The natural growth and development in writing evident in the junior school is not usually replicated in middle-school classrooms. It became apparent that children often were not writing as well in Year Six as they were in Year Three. There was a falling away of development that gave us cause for great concern.

It became obvious that teachers should not expect new forms of writing to develop in the same natural manner. It was not uncommon for middle-standard children to express writing boredom. Only highly imaginative children kept their original enthusiasm. We began to think that this was probably due to the repetitive nature of the writing tasks. As nothing new was being introduced to the writing experiences of the children, it was probably only natural that children would stay with the familiar, and now mundane, topics of previous years.

The familiar was more often than not the narrative and the personal recount. The personal recount was still one of the most common forms of writing at the Year Eight level. (See *The Big Win*.) How much different is this to the example *Snoopy* done by Sonia, a Year Three child?

Avid readers had a range of literary experiences that became models for future stories. Those who did not have this rich literary background tended to re-tell TV and video. In terms of writing development, nothing new was happening. Instead of retelling Rapunzel they now retold last night's video, as shown in the example *The Golden Gun*. Is this much different to the story *Sally and the Witch?*

Free writing
In his address to the New Zealand English Teachers' Conference (Christchurch, 1982) Donald Graves discussed his early attempts at teaching free writing. Graves remarked, 'We had great quantities – just like the city dump.'

Unfortunately New Zealand teachers discovered that free topic choice often delivered the same returns. Older writers commonly used violence and mayhem to secure an audience. These were the unfortunate excesses of process writing.

Grave's (1982) observations of top American teachers of writing showed that 'Eighty per cent of children's topics were self-chosen.' This enabled the teacher to ensure that 20 per cent of the topics were

> **THE BIG WIN**
> Knock–knock–knock. I heard someone knocking at the door. I opened the door and found Jamie standing on the porch. 'Hurry up!' he yelled. I looked at my watch. It said 8.30am. I walked to my room and grabbed my gear ready for our game of basketball. A thought came to my head. If we win our game today we will be the best team in the Otago under 13's. I trudged out the door and we started walking into town ...
> David (Year Eight)

▲ This personal recount is still one of the most common forms of writing used by twelve-year-old students.

> **THE GOLDEN GUN**
> The day was the 8th June 1969. Joe Thompson just got up. It was a warm sunny day outside. He went to the kitchen as usual to have breakfast. His father would be sitting there waiting for him. But today he wasn't there. Joe went looking for him around the house but couldn't find him. He looked outside and noticed the barn door open. He ran and looked inside. Hanging from some rope was his father. Joe stood up and pulled the rope off his father's neck. He ran into the house and got his gun and a box of bullets and rode into town. When he arrived the town was quiet. There was not one single store open and there were no horses. He saw two tall men walking towards him. They were the Logan brothers ....
> Thomas (Age 11 years)

▲ Students without a range of rich literary experiences simply retell stories they have seen on television or video.

> **SALLY AND THE WITCH**
> Once upon a time Sally went for a walk in the forest. All of a sudden she found she was lost. 'What will I do?' said Sally. I will go and ask the way. Just then an old woman came along. 'Are you lost little girl?' said the witch. 'Yes', said Sally. 'You come with me,' said the old witch. So she did.
> Toni (Age 8 years)

▲ Compare this story with *The Golden Gun*. Is there really so much difference between the two?

A Factual Report

SMITH'S FARM
Last Wednesday afternoon Room 7 visited Smith's farm to see some sheep getting shorn. Mr Davidson, Tom's father, is a shearer and had offered to show the class how to shear a sheep. At half past ten the bus arrived and Mr Parkinson told us to line up outside. He reminded us to take our coats and gumboots as the forecast had predicted it would rain, etc.
Brian (Year Six)

▲ A factual report will focus on who, when, where, what, why and how.

A Subject Report

SMITH'S FARM
Smith's farm is a sheep farm located near Wyndham some 25k from Invercargill. It is a small farm, and Mr Smith must also work at the Mataura freezing works to support his family.

The farm has a farm-house, a shearing shed, yards and a tool and implement shed. Mr Smith owns a tractor but usually contracts out any work that requires a lot of machinery, etc.
Brian (Year Six)

▲ This is a subject report. Note that it only records facts about the farm. It **does not** include comment about the class or about other incidents that might have occurred during the visit.

---

directed. He also found that most of the children's self-chosen topics came from the curriculum. This did not happen in New Zealand classrooms where children often had complete freedom of choice.

Writing Across the Curriculum

Our studies showed that many teachers and children became confused during this process writing phase as to what they were trying to achieve. To this day, many do not consider writing in science, health, social studies, etc., as writing. Often we found that process writing methods were used for stories, while more traditional methods were used for curriculum studies.

Children often wrote in books called story (narrative?) books, while more often curriculum writing was copied from reference books or from blackboards. Is it any wonder children become confused? While often encouraged to take risks in process writing, curriculum writing is often expected to be done as a perfect one-off draft. It must be done, of course, 'Neatly, with a nice heading.'

When this is pointed out to teachers they are quick to see merit in trying to keep consistency in approach when teaching different varieties of writing. They usually mention problems faced with scraps of draft writing paper and keeping the drafts in some sort of order. One method that has proved successful is to have children keep all draft writing in one book. Some subject study writing then stays as draft, while other work is fully processed. It is not uncommon for children to be working on several drafts at the same time. Children find this concept easy to handle, and teachers have ready access to a record of all writing.

It also becomes obvious that teachers cannot teach children to write in different genres if they do not themselves know how to construct these texts. For example, I have found few teachers who understand the structures of a factual report. Most get confused with factual reporting as compared to subject reporting. If a class has visited Smith's farm, a news report will focus on who, when, where, what, why and how.

On the other hand, a subject report will focus on the farm and give information about such things as location, size, stock and equipment. The class, children and other incidents will not be part of this text.

When class visits take place it is more likely that children will be asked to recount their personal experiences rather than write a factual report.

A wide range of transactional texts including instructional and explanatory texts, argument, discussion and essay must be developed with these older children. If children are to be successful in higher education they must be able to use their writing as a tool of learning. To do this they must be conversant with a wide range of writing genres and be able to select the correct form with regard to purpose and audience.

Integrating writing across the curriculum

When I first began writing about classroom programmes, my main classroom organisational method was the writing workshop. This method enabled teachers to set in place conferencing routines, allowed for daily writing – something that was not happening at that time – and encouraged children to publish for readers. As mentioned earlier, this led to problems – writing became very narrative-based and there was no carry-over to other curriculum areas.

I now believe that teachers working with children in standard classes must look at integrating writing across the curriculum. There are many reasons for this, but let us consider:

- Pressure of time. The curriculum is now so crowded that finding thirty minutes solely for writing has become most difficult.
- Most writing done by children in the standards is curriculum-based writing. It makes sense to teach specialised forms of writing within the subject area.
- Writing and reading go together. They are like processes requiring the same learning strategies.
- Reading programmes at a senior school are often based on study skills, i.e. the ability to locate, sift, order and use information. Writing is one of the major ways people transact information.

Using the Curriculum

It would seem good sense to use various subject studies to stimulate interest in writing. The reading programme is where children are shown research and study skills. The language programme is a time for writing up the study.

This may mean that for several days, as information is gathered, there would be no writing undertaken. The next several days might find little formal reading instruction as students use the time to write a record of the study. Teachers may set one or two specific learning objectives for each of these areas. Teachers collect data on eight children to evaluate the unit. During the next study, observations are made of a different group. Too often we try to collect data on thirty children at a time. Any data collection tasks should be manageable. We must ask:

- Who do we want to collect data from?
- When are we going to collect it?
- How will we collect it?
- How will we record it?
- Why are we collecting it?
- What are we going to do with it?

The above structure allows teachers to devote more time to teaching research-based learning. If the time spent on unit studies, instructional reading, and writing is blocked, time

---

Topic: Science – Fresh-water Pond

Science Goals
– Children will gain understanding about the variety of life forms that share the fresh-water pond as a common habitat.

Reading Goals
– Children will select appropriate reference books to locate and gather information.
– They will set realistic research questions.
– They will skim-read, note-take and order information.

Writing Goals
– With teacher assistance children will write a formal report about life in a fresh-water pond.
– They will then select one pond creature and attempt to research and, with guidance, write their own independent report.
– Selected children may write independently.
– Some may work in a 'shared' fashion with the teacher.

▲ An example of observation and comment in science. This story was written by a six-year-old.

does not become a problem. If the writing goal is to learn to write scientifically, the time to teach this is surely in science. Correspondingly, science-based information might be collected during reading and language. Time is there to be used creatively.

It might be argued that working in this way takes away learners' freedom of choice. In fact it offers a different range of choices to the learner. For instance, there is choice in selecting an independent pond study. There is choice in the way the research project is set up. There may be choice given the use of the information. This may involve writing a poem, designing a chart, making a series of illustrated observations, writing a narrative or giving an explanation. It is possible to give choice within the framework of a set topic. This choice is only possible when children have gained confidence in writing in a variety of forms.

If teachers believe in the concept of daily free writing, how can this be accommodated in a programme that has several days put aside for research prior to writing? There are several answers to this question.

1. You can't write about nothing. In order to write you have to know your topic. Information gathering, setting a purpose, picking the audience and deciding on the form are major parts of the writing process (see *Dancing with the Pen*, Learning Media (1991), page 23).

2. Children should write freely for at least ten minutes of every day. This may be in a journal or a learning log. As with S.S.R. (Sustained Silent Reading), we should have S.S.W. (Sustained Silent Writing).

3. Within a balanced writing programme there will be a range of other writing opportunities. These may perhaps be found in Shared or Guided writing sessions.

Retaining the Best Aspects of Process Writing

Conferencing

There are many elements of process writing programmes, e.g. the different types of conferencing, that can be adapted to any written language programme. These conferencing techniques must remain part of any organisation. Without regular conferencing sessions children seldom come to understand the revision processes that mark good writing. As Donald Murray said, 'Writing is not writing without revision.' Beginner writers learn this through being exposed to regular writing conferences.

The conferences ensure that children interact with other writers. Writing partners, writing groups, roving teacher conferences and editing conferences are still most important in the developing maturity of the writer. If teachers change programme structures, they must try to keep the peer learning opportunities that are the heart of the writing workshop.

Writing workshops

Emphasis on conferencing does not mean that there is no place for writing workshops. These workshops are probably critical for Year

One to Year Three children as they learn about writing. They are also an excellent starting point for teachers who are learning to teach children how to write. Workshops provide children with opportunities to make discoveries about spelling, and how to communicate with others through their writing. Writing workshops can also teach children to interact with others and to ask questions of ambiguous text. This is the time when young writers learn basic writing strategies.

The requirements of a curriculum versus those of the learner

It saddens me to report that during the last three years I have noted that what I consider to be the foundation of writing teaching – the conferencing strategies – have been sadly neglected. The focus has been shifted heavily towards the teaching of different *genres* and the questioning strategies, fundamental to the development of the independent writer, have been neglected. I believe that this is a downside to work with a prescriptive curriculum. Teachers are now starting to teach towards meeting the objectives of a document rather than meeting the learning requirements of individuals. This is worrying.

Junior and senior school writing

There is a much-quoted saying: 'In the junior school children learn to read. In the senior school they read to learn.' This implies that the junior school teaches the child how to read, and the senior school teaches the child how to take advantage of this ability. The same statement could be made about writing. 'In the junior school children learn to write. In the senior school they write to learn.'

In terms of reading instruction, most teacher interactions are geared towards giving children strategies so they can achieve independence as readers. Usually younger children meet daily with the teacher in a guided reading session. As they become independent, they take over the learning tasks, and the teacher becomes a director, or facilitator, of learning.

The writing workshop could be likened to the guided reading session. The workshop provides teacher support to beginning writers. As children develop basic skills, the teacher gradually builds up other support structures. The class, writing partners and writing groups progressively take over the role of responders to draft text.

By Year Four most children write fluent, if not completely accurate written statements. Although the number of children requiring daily supports starts to decline, some children and teachers may require the workshop structure during the middle school years. The place of conferencing will be explored in greater depth in the chapter entitled 'The Classroom Programme: Leading the Horse to Water'.

As mentioned in an earlier chapter, *Dancing with the Pen* was written as a text about the teaching of writing, not as a text on process writing. The processes had to be given prominence, as this is how writers write. The book endeavours to discuss writing, in a variety of contexts, for a variety of audiences, for a variety of purposes. The processes remain important, and being able to pick the correct written form is one of the more important of the processes.

This page was done as part of a study in social studies by a Year Seven student. The student had researched the topic of sawmilling in the past before starting to write this story. ▼

One morning bright and early I decided I would go to the sawmill with Dad to get some timber for the woolshed Dad wanted to build. Dad got the cart out with the hackney and we set off to the sawmill. We rode for about 4 hours and finally we came to the bush which was alongside the sawmill. We watched the wood pigeons flying from tree to tree and I dreamt I was a wood pigeon flying high in the air, when I was interrupted by a bullocky.

It is my belief that junior school classrooms should allow children to make independent discovery about different genres of writing. Teachers in these classrooms have a responsibility to establish a foundation for their senior colleagues. They should be developing within their pupils the following skills and understandings:
- Writers write to convey meaning.
- Writers make this meaning clear through revision (add on, take out, change).
- Writers will develop a system of spelling (at this time it may not be correct in form).
- Writers will know and use some print conventions (full-stop, etc.).
- Writers will develop motor skills that enable them to write quickly and efficiently.

Donald Graves *Writers – Teachers and Children at Work* (Heinemann)

If children leaving Year Three can develop these understandings, and are able to write a personal recount, make observations and comments about their world, write a simple personal letter and retell a known story, a sound learning foundation has been established. As children are developmentally different, teachers will be expected to provide programmes that meet the needs of the individual.

Writing and Close Reading

The processes of *critical thinking, processing information and exploring language* are developed within the close reading aspect of the writing programme.

Part of the *exploring language* process is understanding different writing structures. The introduction of any new genre is undertaken within the study of how professional writers write: narrative, instructions, explanations, argument, etc. For children to be able to write in these forms, they must understand the structure of text. This happens within the reading programme, not the writing programme. This is explained in more detail on pages 53 and 54 of this text.

After this understanding is implicit, a more structured approach to teaching the genre is possible.

A Planned Method of Genre Development

There is nothing to stop teacher introducing junior school children to a range of different writing genres. In fact, it is quite important that they are exposed to a number of writing forms before they are expected to attempt independent writing.

The method outlined in the chapter 'Shared and Guided Writing' allows for children to be:
- Made aware of a new form via shared writing
- Shown how the form is structured via guided writing.

If junior children have engaged in the shared writing of different non-fiction genres, the senior school teachers can move the child towards independence. First, the teacher will guide the child through the writing of the new form, and then soon after give the child the opportunity to experiment independently through the writing of a similar text.

Many schools are looking at the concept of having a term focus where a different writing genre is highlighted each term. If this is planned to occur during Years Four to Six, children will move into their intermediate schooling with an understanding of nine different writing genres.

It is not possible to cover all these different forms of writing in three years. Teachers will need to be selective, but there are some common rules that cover many of the above forms.

In the chapter entitled 'Monitoring the Individual – Assessing the Curriculum', I have outlined a method that requires different forms of writing to be introduced at one level through shared writing, taught at the next level via guided writing, then consolidated at subsequent levels as children use writing across the curriculum.

Descriptive reports

These start with an opening paragraph that tells about the subject being covered, e.g. 'Fire-fighters are very brave people whose job is to protect the community by fighting fires and saving property.' Information is ordered under subject headings and written in paragraphs. Present tense is always used. The fire-fighters will still be fighting fires tomorrow, so the writer's information can be verified.

Instructional (procedural) texts

- Have a stated goal. 'How to make……….'
- A list of materials.
- Steps to follow. Always starting with the verb…, e.g. Mix…. Cut…. Add…. Walk….

Writing genres in the senior school

These are some of the more important of the writing genres that senior children need to be able to control.

A list of different texts

Poetic	Transactional	Expressive
mystery	directories	journal
science fiction	recipes	diary
adventure	forms	reminders
fairy tale	how to play ...	logs
myths/legends	how to make ...	shopping lists
western	hot to get to ...	plans
folk tale	reports (descriptive)	recounts
fable	reports (news/factual recount)	letters
letter	letter (business)	poetry
video	advertising	jottings
songs	argument	songs
	discussion	

Explanatory texts
- Set the problem. Usually a How or Why statement, e.g. 'How does a jet boat engine work?'
- A paragraph that explains the phenomenon, e.g. 'A jet boat is a boat that uses a jet of water as a means of propulsion.'
- Next the workings of the engine are explained. This explanation is often clarified through the use of diagrams.

Often science experiments use a blend of instructional and explanatory texts to explain experiments.

Narratives
Narratives always have a setting, main character and minor characters. The main character is faced with a problem and the story is complete when this problem is resolved. Many minor problems and resolutions keep the reader interested.

Recounts
Note: There are both 'expressive' and 'transaction' recounts. These are explained fully in the chapter 'Working with the English Curriculum'.

The first paragraph sets out When, Who, Why, Where, How, e.g. 'Last Friday afternoon Room Ten took a bus to the plastic works to see how they make plastic bags.'

The piece will then follow through the events of the visit in chronological order. Words such as Firstly, When, After, Before, As soon as, Soon, etc. show the passing of time.

Children need alternatives to *and then* which is the way young children show the passing of time.

Arguments
Only one side is ever presented when writing an argument. The writer takes a side and defends it.
- State the case. 'Should the Hunting of Whales be Internationally Condoned?'
- Put a point of view. 'I believe that the hunting of whales should …'
- Express the evidence.
- Writers can sum up if they wish.
- Writers have to decide on the other person's arguments and counter these with strong arguments of their own.
- A discussion is different because here the writer presents both sides of a case and leaves it to the reader to decide.
- 'It has been argued …' 'On the other hand …'

Poetry
Teachers are often very keen to have their children write poetry. Often the children have an idea that poetry means 'it has to rhyme'. This is where we get many examples of fat/cat, moon/spoon, look/book type of poetry. Much of it is nonsense.

I believe that looking at form poetry is a good way to introduce children to poetry. Useful examples are the Cinquain and the Haiku.

Both metaphor and simile can be introduced through poetry. The

---

A Cinquain
A five-lined poem. The first line of one word is usually a concept. The last line of five words is a short sentence.

Fear
Suddenly awake
Late at night
Shadows at the window
Head further under my covers.

The Haiku
A poem where the first line contains five syllables, the second line seven and the final line five syllables.

Snow falls in white sheets
Lightly knocking at my door
The wind laughs at me.

The Simile Poem
Using this form, children are encouraged to use similes to describe:

In the early morning
I saw clouds like snow upon the hills.
trees stand like soldiers on parade
cars crawl like beetles along the motorway
From my bedroom window.

simile poem encourages children to describe using similes (see the example given).

The Bio-Poem is useful for character studies in books and also for self-discovery. The form is as follows:
Name
Relationship
Who fears: Three things
Who wishes: Three things
Who wants: Three things
Who would like to be: Three things
Who lives at: Address

Other common form poems such as Acrostic (one line for each letter of the title), Sense poems (tastes like, sounds like, looks like) and Diamond (see example) are also useful form poems to help children develop a variety of language.

This seemingly natural development appears to grow out of children's increasing language maturity and the literacy-based programmes common to junior school classrooms.

Let us leave this section with a word of warning: keep topics manageable.

> **Write about one native bird, not the whole species. Gather data on a limited number of research questions.**

A Plan of Work for Years Four to Six

The following plan looks at what Donald Graves called the '20 per cent' of directed writing. It shows one new focus per team and hopes that children will choose to use these new forms on other occasions during the school year.

It allows for the report to be re-visited each year. This is because the descriptive and report forms are the foundation of most curriculum reports throughout their schooling.

All schools will of course see different needs and requirements for their children. The following is only a suggestion as to how this could be planned.

A school plan for writing

The objective of the term focus (see the plan over page) is to ensure children will have numerous exposures to writing forms in probably four or five teaching sessions during a ten-week block. Some of these specialised forms will be taught in conjunction with specialist subject areas, e.g. recording experiments and explanations in science, instruction in mathematics, etc.

It is expected that all genres developed during Year One to Three will continue to be developed through giving children opportunity to write. Note that there are far fewer examples in this four-year plan than the list given earlier in this chapter. It is better to see children

---

The Diamond Poem
This poem forms the shape of a diamond. It uses the following form:
- A noun
- Two adjectives
- A phrase
- Two adjectives
- A noun

Birds
Bright Quick
Flying high in the clouds
Majestic Graceful
Free

The Bio-Poem
This poem is useful for character studies and self-discovery. It follows a set form.

Jack
Son of the old widow
Who fears: giants, being poor, his mother
Who wishes: he hadn't sold the cow, to be rich, never to be hungry
Who wants: to be successful, wealthy and happy ever after
Who would like to be: a prince, brave, safe
Who lives at Dell Farm
Nursery Rhymeland.

leaving Year Six able to write well in twelve different genres than poorly in many.

At the same time, the class-shared writing programme should be introducing the children to many different writing forms. Some of these forms will be used as an introduction to more structured teaching at a later date. At other times the teacher will demonstrate an uncommon form. The interested child may decide to experiment with this new form. Children should not be closed off from a range of new ideas by the dictates of a school programme.

The New Zealand English Curriculum lists the writing of Poetic (narrative), Transactional (factual) and Expressive (personal) as being major instructional goals. No longer can teachers afford to sit and wait for things to happen. Schools must now be proactive in providing adequate writing programmes. For this to happen teachers must be better trained and prepared.

In the past only a few teachers have been given the opportunity of taking part in written language in-service training. Now more than ever staff must be trained to recognise development progression, and to teach children how to write in a variety of forms. As mentioned earlier, 'You can't teach what you don't know.' School development programmes must be put in place to meet this need.

A SUGGESTED MODEL FOR A SCHOOL WRITING PLAN

Y.4
- TERM 1: Report
- TERM 2: Instructional (How to make)
- TERM 3: Poetry
- TERM 4: Narrative (Adventure)

Y.5
- TERM 1: Report, Explanation (Revisited)
- TERM 2: Factual Account (News report)
- TERM 3: Narrative (Animal story)
- TERM 4: Instructions (How to play)
- Poetry Options

Y.6
- TERM 1: Report (Revisited)
- TERM 2: Factual Report (Revisited); Science Instructions/Explanations (Experiments)
- TERM 3: Argument
- TERM 4: Video (Writing & production)
- Poetry Options

School Review: Questions to Ask

- [ ] Do our teachers hold a common philosophy as to how children learn to write?

- [ ] Is there a common set of teaching procedures used throughout the school?

- [ ] Have all staff had recent in-service training and are they up-to-date with current theory?

- [ ] Do teachers monitor children against the writing behaviours of the emergent, early and fluent writer?

- [ ] Can they explain differences in these developmental bands to a parent?

- [ ] Are teachers aware of current research into developmental spelling?

- [ ] Could teachers view a spelling sample and be able to analyse it and state the next learning step?

- [ ] Is there a common view held about the need for child proofreading?

- [ ] Is there a common child-centred recording system that focuses on what the learner can do?

- [ ] Do teachers write <u>to</u> and <u>with</u> their pupils?

- [ ] Do teachers articulate the forms of different writing genres?

- [ ] Is there a school policy as to how different genres will be introduced to children?

- [ ] Do teachers use draft writing books and learning journals?

- [ ] Is there evidence that children understand the revision process?

- [ ] Is there evidence that at least 10% of Year Six (Std. 4) children engage in self-questioning of text and have a range of strategies to independently revise their text?

- [ ] Is the writing process used across the curriculum? Do the children have the necessary study skills to make this an achievable goal?

- [ ] Do children use the language of the writer, i.e. do they discuss drafts, revision, proofreading, audience, webbing, etc.?

- [ ] Can writing progress and development be seen clearly across the school?

- [ ] Does each area of the school have a clear sense of purpose and vision in their teaching?

The following chapters will endeavour to cover some of the points that schools need to consider if they are to develop successful writing programmes and create successful writers.

4

In this chapter

- **Developing a balanced writing programme**
- **Shared and guided reading and writing**
- **Shared writing**
- **Guided writing**
- **Guided reading and writing: comprehension and meaning**
- **Writing a report**
- **Lesson samples**

Shared and Guided Writing

In *Dancing with the Pen*, we mentioned the need to have a balanced writing programme. To try to explain our thinking, we need to revisit our New Zealand philosophy. This philosophy stresses the need to have a balance of:
- Reading to children.
- Reading with children.
- Reading by children.

In our efforts to make use of this sound reading philosophy, we decided to base our text on:
- Writing to children.
- Writing with children.
- Writing by children.

In the past, most children have been expected to learn to write through independent writing; that is, the instructional method focused on writing by children. Pupils were given topics and expected to produce pieces of written work, but seldom were they adequately instructed as to how different types of text were written.

Reading instruction has relied on an entirely different approach. It would be unheard of for teachers not to read to their children every day. It is also well understood that when text is too difficult for children, shared or guided reading approaches are used. Our writing team believed that it was important that the same approaches be used to introduce children to new writing challenges.

Developing a Balanced Writing Programme

Let us consider the reasons for having balance in the reading programme and then explore the need to develop this same balance within the writing programme.

Teachers know that it is important that children engage in daily reading. The 'reading by' and 'writing by' methods have always been given pride of place when teaching children to read and write. It has been commonly said, 'You learn to read by writing.' While this philosophy is still sound, the last twenty years have witnessed major changes in the ways children are taught to read. The concepts of *to*, *with* and *by* have brought about a balancing of instructional techniques.

Models for children

Teachers have always read to their children. In some cases this might have been viewed as a means of keeping children entertained, or filling

in the odd five minutes before lunch, but most teachers understand there are wider educational reasons for reading to children on a daily basis. We now understand that reading to children:
- demonstrates how adults read
- enables the child to listen to oral phrasing
- develops an understanding of, and love of, good literature
- develops comprehension
- shows that the teacher values reading.

Current research shows that many children are not seeing adult teachers as reading role models. Also, more often than not, adult reading does not take place in front of children. In the past, reading was one of the major ways people entertained themselves. Now with TV, videos, electronic games, computers, etc., people are not spending as much time reading.

There is a body of research that leads us to believe that children see more women readers than men. Some children, boys in particular, may tend to view reading as a female trait if they do not have male role models.

The same is probably true when we consider children's opportunities to view adult writers. Children are probably more likely to see the mother as a writer than the father. Some fathers do bookwork at home, but often this is done later at night. Once again, it is possible that at home some boys view writing as a female occupation. Mothers write letters, shopping lists, recipes, notes, etc., and it is usually on these forms of writing that young children base their observations. Unfortunately it is most likely to be the girls in the family who seem to have most opportunities to make these observations. Boys are more likely to be outside playing, or, as in many parts of Southland, helping Dad work with the sheep.

Our observations of new entrants suggest that it is more likely girls will develop an early understanding of how writing works. Many have had prior experience of caption copying. It is not therefore surprising that they often regard themselves as copiers rather than writers. Many are quite proficient at this activity.

Some children have never seen their parents write, while many have never been given pencil and paper as a play-thing. These children really stand out, as often they are at a loss as to what is expected of them. The more intelligent of this group quickly look at what other children are doing and copy.

Shared and Guided Reading and Writing

Shared and guided reading
Shared reading approaches have been widely used to introduce children to text. When texts are too difficult for the child, shared reading is the only appropriate teaching strategy. The child is gradually encouraged to read along with the teacher, possibly a couple of beats behind, and to follow the written text. This technique is used with people of all ages if the text is too difficult.

This shared approach makes the text accessible to the child. It develops interest in reading. Interesting stories are selected that have a degree of repetition in their text. Children are encouraged to invent their reading as they try to reproduce this shared activity.

As with shared reading, guided reading is also used to make text accessible to children. It is used when children have acquired a number of reading and language skills. Students are then able to make their own attempts at decoding text.

In both cases the teacher has an important role, but where the teacher is doing most of the decoding in shared reading, the child is expected to take a greater role in guided reading.

Shared and guided writing

Let us now see how these approaches apply in the teaching of writing. To understand shared and guided writing, we first need to understand how the two approaches differ.

Modelling or demonstration?

Shared writing is based on a philosophy of **demonstration** while guided writing is based on a philosophy of **modelling**. What is the difference? Harste, Short and Burke, in their book *Creating Classrooms for Authors* (Heinemann, 1988), explain it thus:

> Demonstration is not modelling. A careful look at instances of learning that some people call modelling will reveal that the child has not imitated or modelled everything present.

An example of this type of modelling is when teachers supply a caption to be copied or a corrected text to be transposed during publishing. Even then, how often is this correctly reproduced?

The authors express a belief that learners attend only to the demonstrations that hold meaning for them at that point of time relative to their stage of development. No one attends to all demonstrations that are present in a communicative event. Gardiner (1980) explained demonstration in this way:

> Attention to demonstrations is generative. It is a means of learning how something might be done rather than how it must be done.

And finally, once again to quote Harste, Short and Burke:

> Children should be invited to, rather than forced to engage in specific literacy activities.

Teachers therefore provide demonstrations as to how successful language learners solve problems. I would put forward the thesis that when we use shared writing approaches we are demonstrating, but when we guide children's writing we are modelling. The outcomes from both will be entirely different. For the pupil, shared writing is open-ended, while guided writing will see some reproduction of the form modelled.

Shared Writing

The earliest forms of shared writing used in junior school programmes are the charting of oral language experiences. Here the teacher uses writing to record visits, activities, thought, etc. The children frame up the text and the teacher acts as scribe. This approach is more often than not regarded as a reading activity, but in fact is a very powerful way of demonstrating the links between spoken and written text.

Another activity, used from the first day in many New Zealand classrooms, is 'Newsboard'. Here children's oral news is recorded on a large sheet of newsprint. Children are invited to circle known words and letters. Children engage in a range of language forms including word building, compound words, contract words, punctuation, grammar, parts of speech and other language rules and conventions. The teacher is free to select any skill that is thought to be appropriate to the age group.

The philosophy of this approach relies heavily on teacher demonstration. The children are expected to take responsibility for their own learning and no mastery is expected. It is, however, interesting to see how quickly children develop a high-frequency vocabulary and learn many rules of language without any formal teaching. Some examples of shared writing experiences are provided at the end of this chapter.

Working with junior writers

The chapter in this book dealing with monitoring the curriculum suggests the following approach to introduce students to new forms of writing. The new form is initially shared at one level, guided at

Figure 4.1
A Comparison of Shared and Guided Writing
These pie graphs illustrate how responsibility for writing moves from the teacher to the child as each new approach is introduced.

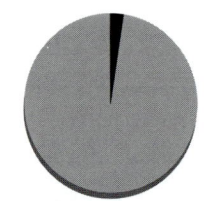

■ Teacher
■ Child

Writing to
The child as observer.

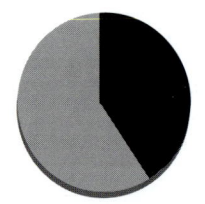

Shared
The teacher does most of the work. The child participates.

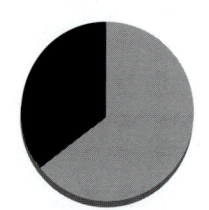

Guided
The child does most of the work. The teacher guides.

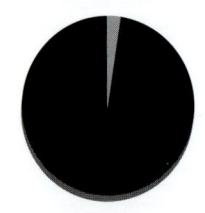

Writing by
The child as writer. The teacher is an observer.

the following level and then children are expected to consolidate the form as they write within the curriculum.

Junior school children may be introduced to a range of different genres through this shared writing approach. There is a danger, however, in trying to formalise many different forms at an early stage of their writing development. These children have so many new things to learn that over-teaching of different writing forms is unnecessarily demanding. At the same time, through shared writing, the bright child quickly develops an understanding of the unfamiliar forms and their likely audiences. Often these children pick up many of these forms without formal teaching. Year Four is quite early enough to start more formalised instruction. By that time most children have established the basics of writing and have a natural understanding of a variety of the more common genres.

Guided Writing

The method discussed is often called 'scaffolding'; that is, as the child becomes more proficient the scaffolding is gradually removed and the child takes over ownership.

When introducing any new writing genre to the class, the first approach should be a shared writing approach where the teacher and class plan and write together, the teacher being the final scribe.

The next approach is the guided approach where the teacher and children plan together, but the children construct their own piece. This may be built up in sections, e.g. if we were researching native birds and had collected our information, we might want to construct a number of reports. Perhaps, having written a number of shared reports on other subjects, the teacher might decide to guide children through the writing of a report. Having selected the fantail, it might be decided that the report should be constructed in the following manner:
- Opening statement (telling about and defining the fantail).
- Paragraphs covering appearance, habitat, breeding.
- Teacher leads children through each step, but each child writes independently.
- The next step is for children to take another native bird and work through the task independently.

Current research by Australian educational consultants such as Beverley Derewianka, stresses that children may be aware of the genre, but may not yet be confident enough to write the text independently. It stresses the need for some children to be supported through cycles of learning (Fig. 4.2). They might need to repeat these cycles several times before becoming confident enough to take control. Refer to Example 4, Modelling the Report, as an example of learners being supported through cycles of learning.

New entrants probably need a lot of guided writing as they struggle to master the skills of inventive spelling. As they acquire this skill the teacher's presence becomes less important. The teacher gradually withdraws and allows the child to take over the task.

Guided Reading and Writing: Comprehension and Meaning

As time passes guided reading remains an important part of classroom reading programmes. Comprehension now becomes the driving force of these lessons, and reasoning and discussion are undertaken in greater depth.

Too often guided reading lessons in the junior school are directed towards decoding skills, and often discussion and reasoning are of only secondary consideration. This highlights why easily read text should be chosen for these lessons. Discussion and reasoning only take place when children can read the text easily.

The same is true of guided writing approaches. When the children understand the text – construction, reason, audience, method – teachers can give more attention to the finer details of comprehension and reasoning. The revision processes then have meaning for children, as they are secure in their ability to construct the text.

Often children who are considered to be slow learners find this type of writing – especially the transactional forms – most rewarding. The children are writing to pass on information, and therefore the writing has to be clear and precise. If they know the topic, the form, and have some reasonable spelling skills, they can become proficient writers of non-fiction. You do not have to have a great command of language or vivid imagination to construct a clear factual report.

Close reading

The national curriculum demands that teachers undertake *close reading* as a major part of their reading programmes. The three areas of study are:
Critical Thinking
Exploring Language
Processing Information.

I would see *critical thinking* of text as something to be explored as children engage in guided silent reading. Children are talked through the text and are shown the sorts of questions that mature readers ask during reading. This would always be my initial guided lesson with any text. Comprehension must always be established before exploring the text further.

The exciting part of close reading is that the text can be revisited for a variety of purposes. On revisiting the text on another occasion, children and teacher might discuss the structure of the text and the language choices made by the author. This exploring language activity means that children can see how professional writers construct text. For example, discussion might focus on:
- setting
- main character introduced
- minor characters introduced
- problem signalled
- story unfolds problem/resolution until such time as major problem is resolved. This is often called the 'climax'
- story rounded off to the satisfaction of the reader.

Figure 4.2
Shared or Guided Writing Cycles
As children move through each cycle of learning, they need to be supported. Some children might need to repeat these cycles several times before becoming confident enough to reach the independent stage.

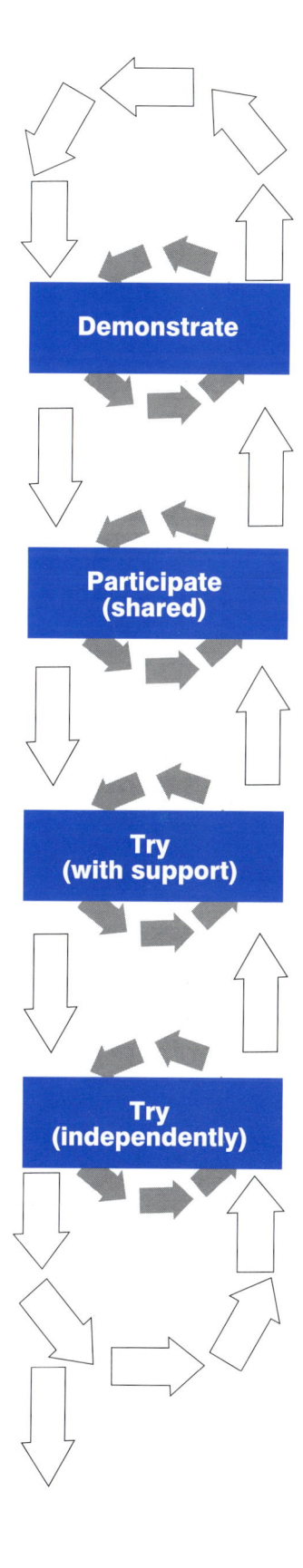

- Demonstrate
- Participate (shared)
- Try (with support)
- Try (independently)

Fire Fighters

Fire fighters are people that risk their own lives to save other people. They put out fires in public buildings, like libraries and schools and they also attend fires in homes.

They wear fireproof coats and trousers which are mostly yellow. This colour is chosen for the clothing because it can be seen easily. They also wear red hats which have special plastic down the front to guard their faces from the smoke and heat. They first put their boots on and then they put their trousers on. The trousers have to be nice and long so that it looks like they are connected to the boots so that the legs can be protected from the flames. Last of all they put their hats on.

The fire fighters use breathing apparatus to help them breathe in the smoke. They have a little timer on the breathing apparatus so they know when they have to get out of the building to get some more oxygen. They have little axes to break windows and glass doors to let some smoke out so that it is easier to breathe. They use these things that are a little like jaws in recovering people. They are called the jaws of life. They are used to rip the roofs off cars to save the lives of people.

The fire engine carries all the gear that the fire fighters will use. It also has a pump on the back that pumps the water into the hoses. The pump has a filter on it. The fire fighters also have three other filters to use when they are getting water from a creek or river. This makes it nice and clean. The fire fighters check the pump once a week to check that it is in order. The fire engine has four different sirens. They also carry one or two stretchers.

▲ This is an example of a report. Refer to Example 4 on page 59 for further detail on how a report such as this can be developed.

The teacher might focus on aspects of descriptions within the story: how the setting or characters are described, the use of adjectives within the writing of descriptions, and what makes these descriptions memorable. This brings the study of elements of language such as parts of speech, use of adverbials, metaphor, simile, personification, analogy, synonyms, antonyms and sentence construction into a real learning context. Hopefully, children will not only expand their knowledge of the English language, but take this language and make it their own during writing.

If children can understand how these forms are constructed, the shared sessions undertaken with the teacher are likely to be more meaningful.

The final part of close reading focuses on processing information. This requires children to make use of the information they have gathered from their reading. This will lead into the teaching of a range of study skills. These are likely to include: question-setting, skim-reading, note-taking and summarising, to name but a few. The acquisition of these skills will likely lead to the children using these skills to gather information prior to engaging in cross-curriculum writing.

Writing a Report

After constructing several reports with the teacher as scribe, children have some idea of the form, but as yet have not attempted to write a report independently. This activity is the link between shared writing of reports and independent report writing. In this activity the teacher will guide the class through the construction of a report.

In his text *Investigating Non-fiction* (Heinemann, 1988), Donald Graves says that when introducing children to report writing, one should pick a topic that the children already know a lot about. He believes it is far better to know too much about a topic than to know too little.

If the goal is for children to use the report form to transact information, it is not desirable to expect them to engage in major research. They would then be expected to master a number of possibly new processes at the same time. The teacher's role is to teach a specialised writing skill. It is best to teach one thing at a time and the teacher must decide the current teaching focus.

In this text I have given the example of writing a report about *Fire Fighters*. (Example 4 at the end of this chapter.)

The children were asked to write their opening statement. This statement would define the term 'fire fighters'. As the children attempted to write their statement, the teacher made a circuit of the classroom. Any children who seemed totally lost were taken to the front of the room where they helped the teacher construct a shared opening statement. These children were brought back to shared writing because the task was obviously beyond their capabilities.

The next step was to decide the next paragraph. In Example 4, the children selected the subject heading *Their Work*. The children were encouraged to write their second paragraph. The shared group tried to work out how this could be recorded, while the teacher made a second circuit of the class. The purpose of this circuit was to identify those children who were finding the task too easy. The teacher then returned to the shared group and helped them with the writing of the second paragraph.

After the teacher and children shared their attempts, the teacher identified the group of fluent writers. They were offered the opportunity of writing the last two paragraphs at their own pace. The rest of the class were taken through the remaining material paragraph by paragraph. Thus there were three types of writing operating in that classroom:
1. Shared Writing – with the teacher
2. Guided Writing – paragraph by paragraph
3. Independent Writing – by those who understood what to do.

During the rest of the semester the class would undertake a number of these sessions working on this genre. It was expected that by the end of the ten-week period there would be a few requiring shared demonstrations and a small group that would require guided writing, while most would now be able to write independently in that particular genre.

As mentioned earlier, it is most important that schools do not jump from one genre to another without giving the children time to consolidate new learning. While this type of approach may be satisfactory for the more able students, average-to-slower children are likely to become confused. Teachers should give children time to acquire new writing skills. At the same time, schools must have a programmed introduction of genres so that nothing is left to chance.

It is expected that soon after the above writing experience, children would be given the opportunity to try out this form on a topic of their own choice. They should try to write the text independently. Some will need to be recycled through the above sequence many times before becoming confident in independent construction. This approach should be considered whenever children are encountering a genre for the first time.

Report or article?

One point of confusion is the usage of the term *report* when talking about the type of writing described above. Some teachers use the term *article* because they use *report* when talking about writing for the newspaper. Most reports written for newspapers are actually factual recounts. Usually they answer the following questions: Who? When? Where? What? Why? Which and How? The first paragraph orients the reader and recounts the events.

Subsequent paragraphs give more detail, opinions from eye witnesses, and may make comment on likely outcomes. The factual recount is an important writing form and needs to be taught. Shared and guided writing techniques enable this teaching to take place.

Some Key Conclusions

The same teaching strategies used to introduce and support children in their reading of unfamiliar text should be used to introduce children to unfamiliar writing forms.

These strategies are: writing *to* children, *with* children and eventually *by* children.

Demonstration and modelling are different processes.

Children learn how to write when they can participate in constructing text with an experienced writer.

Some children need to go through the cycle of *to* and *with* many times before they are capable of independent writing.

The final outcome should be children who are confident and able to write in a range of different genres.

| Example 1 | Shared Writing Experience |

Goal
To teach children how to plan and write a recount of a shared classroom experience.

Objectives
- Children will take part in the shared planning and writing of a common experience.
- Children will construct a plan of a personal experience. They will then discuss the plan with their neighbour.
- Children will write a recount of the experience from their plan.

Method
- Taking a common experience, the teacher suggests that the class should write a record of the event.
- Show children how to write a *story web* getting children to recall the sequence of the experience. Teacher scribes the incidents around the web.
- A second method may be shown, e.g. a *picture web* where the same experience is recalled by drawing a series of small pictures.
- Teacher asks children to try out a good opening sentence in their draft writing books. These are then shared and the teacher uses the children's ideas to construct a statement focusing on when, where, who, what, why, how.
- With the help of the children the teacher uses the story web to construct the rest of the piece. (This may be done over several days, and need not be undertaken in one sitting.)
- Finally, the effort is read and children are then encouraged to plan a personal experience using the same method.
- Children share the plan with a neighbour before attempting to write their experience.

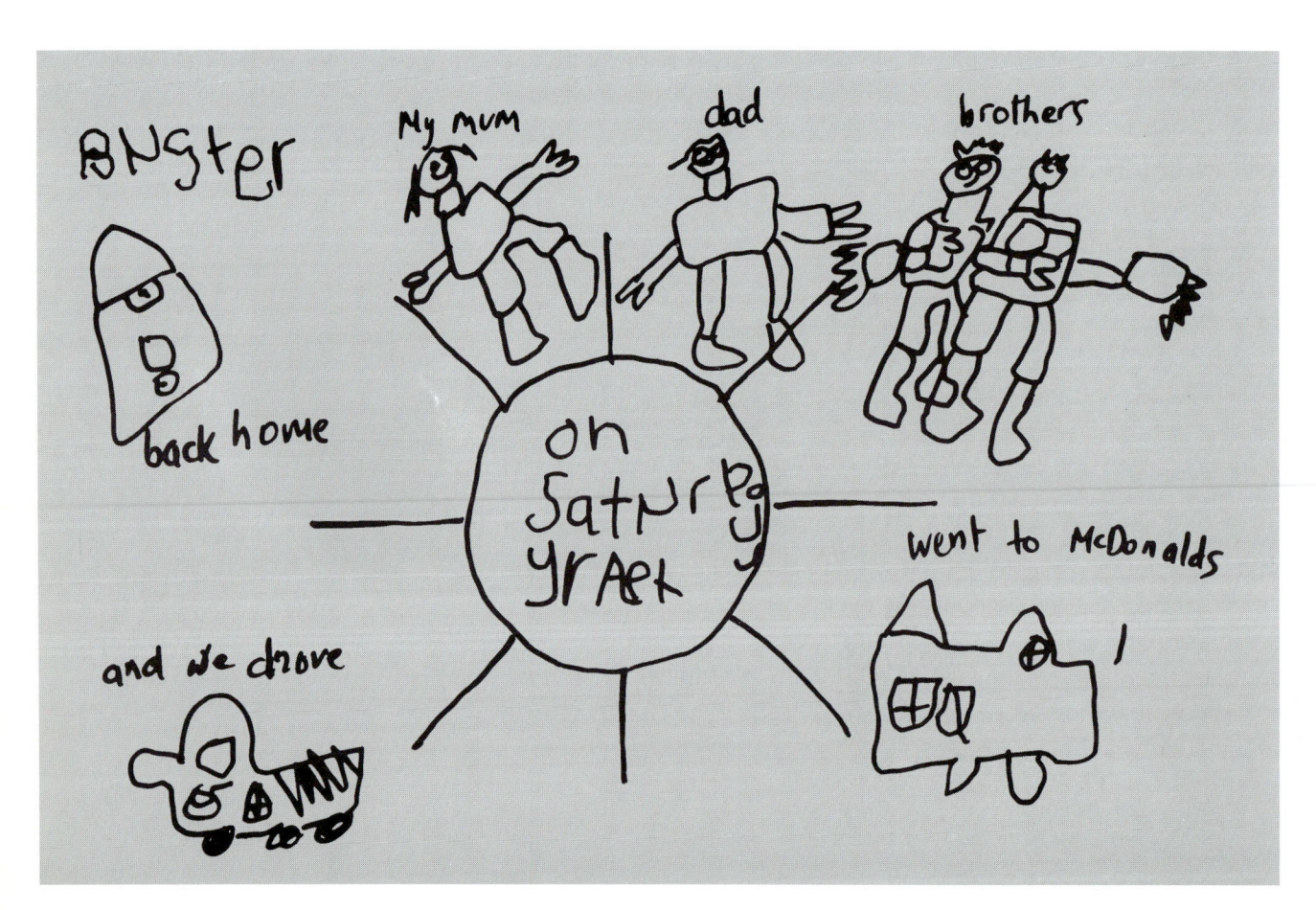

| **Example 2** | **Shared Writing Experience** |

Goal
To aid recall of a known story and study how the narrative genre is constructed.

Objectives
- Children will construct a story web.
- Children will engage in discussion about characters, settings, problems and resolutions within the story.
- Children will construct a collaborative wall story.

Method
- Tell a story to the children. Discuss where the story is set, who the main character is and other characters who play an important part in the story. Identify main problems and resolution.
- Aid children's recall of the story and demonstrate the construction of a story web.
- Children select part of the story to illustrate using paint or crayon.

The first time teachers use this activity it is best to use a shared writing technique. Allow children to try to draft a few sentences that will go with each section. Teacher scribes final product. On subsequent occasions when this method is used, a more guided approach is appropriate. Children write a draft with their picture. Proofread, edit and publish.
- Put published pieces together with pictures and retell the original story.
- Revise characters, problems, etc.
- Publish as a wall story. This later can be taken down and republished as a big book.

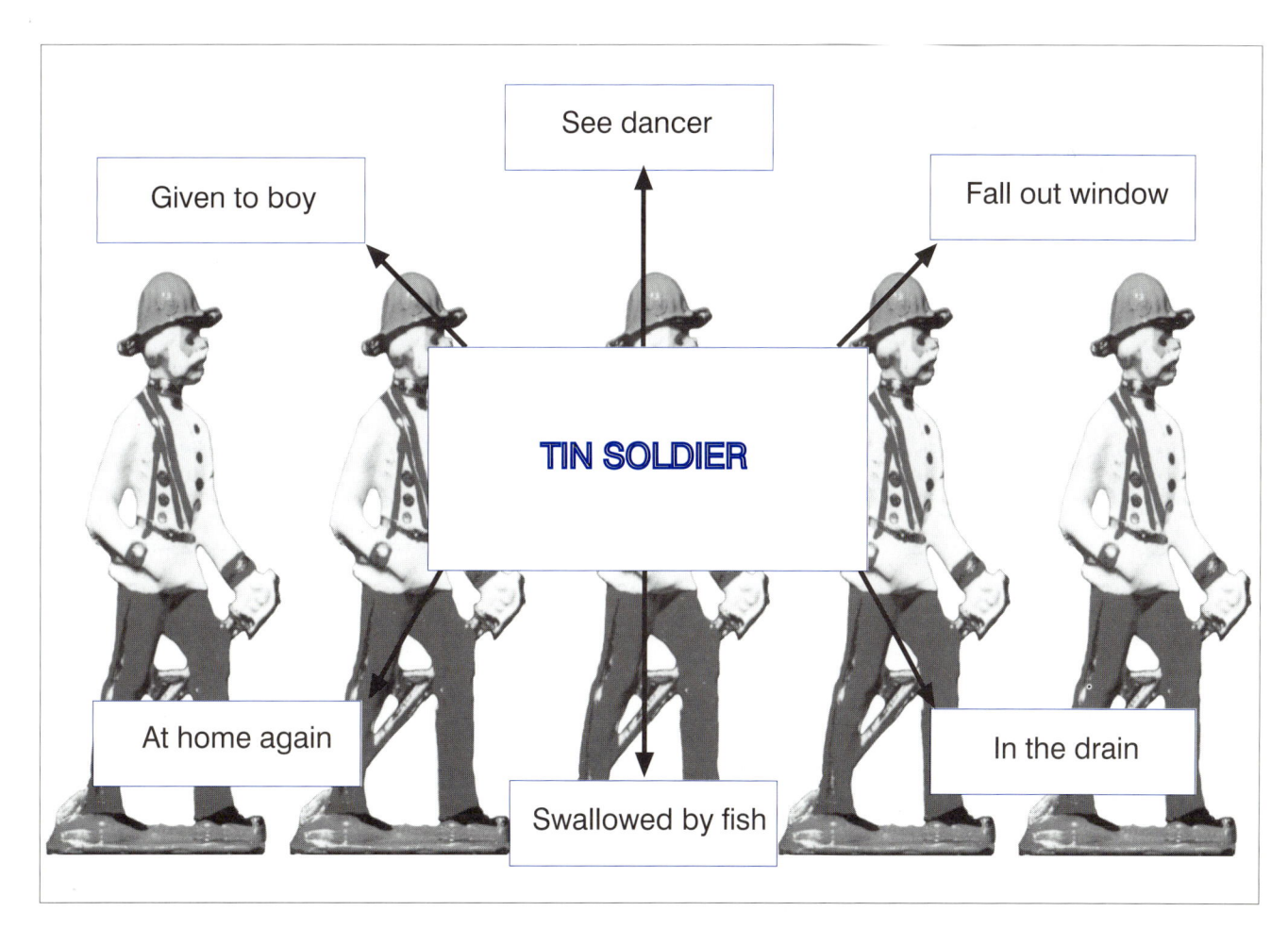

TIN SOLDIER

- Given to boy
- See dancer
- Fall out window
- At home again
- Swallowed by fish
- In the drain

Example 3 Shared Writing Experience

Goal
To introduce children to the revision process using a shared writing approach.

Objectives
- Children will ask questions of text.
- Children will make attempts at writing descriptions.
- Children will engage in the revision of teacher text.
- Children will take part in the construction of a narrative plot line.

Method
- Teacher writes an opening statement. (See below.)
- Teacher says. 'You are my readers. What would you want to know that I have not yet told you?'
- Children usually say, 'You haven't told us what he could see as he looked through the valley.'
- Teachers says, 'O.K. open your draft books. You have three minutes. Tell me what you think he could see.'
- Children write, then read back their pieces to a neighbour. Children are then given the opportunity to share with the class.
- Teacher borrows ideas and shows how these ideas can be added into the text.
- Teacher reads back the first paragraph. Focuses on some words and tries to improve (selects more appropriate) wording. This is probably enough for one session.

Opening statement
David peeped over the cliff at the boat below. It was a wooden boat with tall masts. Ropes hung from the sails. A black flag flew from the mast.

Subsequent sessions
- Work through each part of the statement as mentioned above.
- Teacher says, 'I'm not sure what is going to happen in this story. What do we have to consider? Let's list them.
- Who is David? Why is he in the forest? What problem will he face?
- What other characters are needed? How will the problem be resolved?'
- Class helps teacher construct a plot line.

Plot outline
Sees pirates ➡ Warns village ➡ Fight pirates on beach ➡ Pirates sail away

- Teacher and class build up narrative. (Teacher can pre-write sections of the narrative and present it to the class for comment and revision. This is a good approach if the teacher wants to move the project along if it is 'losing altitude' and needs to be brought in to a landing.)
- Sessions with the children should not take longer than ten minutes at any one time.

David peeped over the cliff at the ship below.

It was a wooden boat with great tall masts. Sails hung limply at the masts and David noted the signs that the boat had lately been in a heavy storm. Rigging was broken and sails were ripped and torn.

Already the crew was busily lowering a boat.

The captain stood on the deck shouting out orders.

He was a big man all dressed in black. Great red whiskers glowed in the morning sun, and David could tell he was very tall as he stood head and shoulders above the rest of the crew.

Example 4 — Modelling the Report

Goal
Children will write a factual report using the correct form.

Objectives
- Children will classify known information under subject headings.
- Children will write a clear opening statement and construct other paragraphs around the known information.
- Children will write in the present tense.
- The information will be clear and logically presented.

Method
- Select a subject that children know quite a bit about.
- In groups record all the knowledge they have.
- Look for likely topic headings and classify.
  (If the group was going to use this as a research project, knowledge would be recorded under the heading 'What we think we know about …'. Groups would then decide on four/five – depending on age – research questions. These would be shared with class. Research would then take place to answer these questions, hopefully confirming our prior knowledge as the subject develops. The Graves method then suggests that each child writes a ten-minute letter to a friend about the topic before using the information in a report form.)
- Children try out an opening statement defining the subject.
- Select order of topics to construct the body of the report. (See web below.)
- Children work through, paragraph by paragraph, reading to a neighbour, questioning, revising under teacher guidance.
- Work may stay in draft, or may be proofread, edited or published if desired.

Web

- Opening Statement
- Their Work
- **FIREFIGHTER**
- Fire Station
- Equipment

FIRE FIGHTERS

Fire fighters are people that risk their own lives to save other people. They put out building fires and fires in public buildings, like libraries, schools and city fires. They also attend private fires like homes and personal property.

They wear fireproof coats and trousers which are mostly yellow. This colour is chosen for the clothing because it can be seen easily. They also wear a red hat which is special plastic down the front to guard their faces from the smoke and heat. They first put their boots and then they put their trousers on. The trousers have to be nice and long so that it looks like they are connected to the boots so that the legs can be protected from the flames. Last of all they put their hat on.

The fire fighters use breathing apparatus to help them breathe in the smoke. They have a little timer on the breathing apparatus so they know when they have to get out of the building to get some more oxygen. They have little axes to break windows and glass doors to let some smoke out so that it is easier to breathe. They use these things that are a little like jaws in recovering people. They are called the jaws of life. They are used to rip the roofs off cars to save the lives of people.

The fire engine carries all the gear that the fire fighters will use. It also has a pump on the back that pumps the water into the hoses. The pump has a filter on it. The fire fighters also have three other filters to use when they are getting water from a creek or river. This makes it nice and clean. The fire fighters check the pump once a week to check that it is in order. The fire engine has four different sirens. They also carry one or two stretchers.

5

In this chapter

- The teacher and the writer
- The questioning chain
- The writing partner
- The group conference
- Self-conferencing
- Proofreading and editing
- Using the 'I Can' Lists
- Publishing

The Classroom Programme: Leading the Horse to Water

If we can keep only one thing in mind – and I fail in this half the time – it is that we are teaching the writer and not the writing.
Lucy Calkins, The Art of Teaching Writing, Heinemann, 1986.

So easy to say; so hard to do. Lucy Calkins knows, through years of experience, that teachers are at heart meddlers. Usually they meddle with all the right intentions, believing that their little suggestions really do improve children's writing. Many probably believe that children are grateful for this assistance. The reality is that children are just too polite, or frightened, to object. Imagine you were the young Samoan child who wrote this piece:

After school I took a short cut through the bushes when I saw a little bird on the grass chirping hard. I ran up to it but it didn't move. Sorrow came to me and I knew it was dying. I thought there was nothing I could do but something came to my mind. I picked it up in my handkerchief and wrapped it up. The bird was brown and white and it had sharp looks with its eyes.

How would you feel if you had to stand and watch it being pulled apart: the teacher deciding how it could be improved? Donald Graves talked about the well meaning teachers who 'wipe out the voices' of would-be writers. In this 1982 research, Graves interviewed thirty-five professional writers. Not one said they had learned to write in school. Most mentioned having their personalities violated and their voices wiped out by interfering teachers.

Sylvia Ashton-Warner wrote in *Teacher* (Virago Ltd, 1980):
When we criticise the contents of the writing, we criticise the contents of their minds.

Her belief was that children cannot control what is in their minds: 'It's just there.' Sometimes teachers try to make the child's mind match theirs. In the end, who owns the writing?

Calkins remarked that teachers are not paid to produce better bulletin boards. Their task is to produce better writers. These writers should eventually become independent enough to write, day in, day out, without the assistance of a teacher. Her message to teachers: teach to empower.

Most teachers still find this concept difficult. This is not surprising, as most teachers have been conditioned by years of what I now call 'negative education'. What do I mean by this?

I have had over forty years of involvement in education: as a pupil, teacher and parent. Most of my classroom learning experiences, my classroom teaching and the learning experiences of my children have been based on a negative philosophy of learning. I well remember my teachers 'red lining' all my errors, and when I started teaching, I worked in exactly the same way. My children, now in their twenties, remember the same things. Even today, when I see a spelling mistake, I want to get in there and obliterate.

My early experience of teaching could be equated with gardening. I was like the gardener who becomes offended at finding a weed in the middle of a newly sown lawn. He becomes obsessed with freeing that lawn of weeds. Others might stand back and view the lawn in context along with the shrubs, flowers, fences and house. Our gardener, however, only sees the lawn and the weeds.

Many people reason that their lawns will always have some flat weeds, some moss and perhaps some daisies. Their object in having a lawn is to keep the property tidy and set off the larger shrubs and trees. It is the total picture that counts. The lawn is just a part of the whole.

My 1994 research of children and their writing tended to suggest that most children see their writing in terms of spelling, punctuation and handwriting. The concept of having something worthwhile to say, and being able to say it in a voice that reflects the personality of the writer does not seem to be commonly understood by student writers.

It would seem that the hidden messages given to children still revolve around accuracy of spelling and surface features. Meaning comes, if at all, far down the list. Teachers are still looking for the weeds before standing back and viewing the whole.

For many, teaching writing is still very much like gardening. Our keen gardener is dedicated to looking after his garden, and it prospers. Other less dedicated gardeners grow weeds. If our gardening friend was a teacher he would be running up and down the block weeding everyone's garden and, as is human nature, most would probably enjoy sitting back watching him at his work.

Earlier in this text, I gave information regarding the *1999 NEMP Writing Tests* and the data regarding children and the revision process. I am very concerned that schools are becoming so intent on the teaching of genre that the strategies required to be a writer are being overlooked. This must not be allowed to happen!

As already mentioned, meaning and clarification of meaning must be the first task of the writer. To teach this to the child, teachers must learn how to work with the text and its meaning.

The Teacher and the Writer

All good teaching is based on routine. Children need to know exactly what will happen when a teacher arrives to respond to a piece. Most of the teachers who have learned to respond effectively to children and their writing have used the following routine, first developed by Graves:
1. The child speaks first. They have to give the teacher the following information:
   - this is what the piece is about
   - this is what I am currently doing
   - this is what I need assistance with.

2. The teacher tries to respond to the problem.

3. The teacher asks, 'What will you do next?'

An example:

Michael I'm writing about the White Pointer. I've got all my information and I've made out a plan, but I'm not sure if I'm including enough information.

Teacher Let me see your plan. Explain it to me.

Michael Well, I thought I might have an opening paragraph about the White Pointer explaining why they are different to other sharks, and a bit about their reputation. Then I thought I might have paragraphs about breeding, habitat, appearance. Or, I might put appearance first. I'm not sure of the order, or if I need other paragraphs.

Teacher The order is really over to you. Appearance might be a good lead in after the general paragraph. You might like to try out both on pieces of paper. You can always cut and paste. What other paragraphs have you considered?

Michael I had thought of doing something about famous White Pointer attacks in New Zealand and Australia. Perhaps something about their life cycle: maybe something about fishing for sharks.

Teacher You seem to have doubts about including these. Why?

Michael I thought the 'attacks' part might be too long: the same for the 'fishing' part. I could include the life cycle under 'breeding'.

Teacher I agree. I think you could have a number of different articles there, Michael. They all seem to have a different purpose. So, what do you think you will do now?

Michael I think I'll stay with what I had and try out the order later.

Usually when I work with children, I try to kneel down and look at the writer and forget the writing. I let the writer read to me, rather than read the writing myself. In this way I don't get side-tracked. You can't see spelling errors unless you look at the print.

If the first comment a teacher makes is about a spelling error children will soon decide that is what a teacher values in a writer. On many occasions I have asked children to identify their best piece of writing and give reasons why. Usually the given reasons are:
- there are not many spelling errors
- it's neat
- I tried hard. It's long.

Good writers are continually engaging in dialogue with themselves. They talk backwards and forwards to themselves first as the storyteller, then as the story reader. They adjust and add meaning. They look for the word and the phrase that will best convey their meaning. They self-conference.

The aim of school programmes should be to produce writers who can engage in this self-conference. If schools can develop this ability in at least the top ten per cent of their most able senior children, they can claim they provide successful writing programmes. Children should be able to add to text, insert into text and delete from text without teacher intervention.

Sadly, such schools are few and far between. John Heenan, now retired from his position as principal of Waihopai School in Invercargill, believed in what he called a 'Questioning Chain'. He believes that if this chain is broken, the school would not see evidence of self-conferencing from their more able senior students.

The Questioning Chain

Heenan believes that children had to be placed in experiences that showed readers desired information from text. He believes learner writers need this experience from their first day at school. The first links in Heenan's chain are the class and the teacher.

The class and the teacher

The first writings done by children should be shared with the class.

Mary stands up and reads.

Mary	My Mum got a new baby.
Teacher	Has anyone got a question for Mary?
Manu	What is it?
Mary	It's a boy.
Toni	What is his name?
Mary	His name is Shane.

The next time the teacher works with Mary.

Teacher	Tell me about your picture Mary.
Mary	This is Shane playing.
Teacher	And this is what you have written down here?
Mary	Yes. Shane is playing.
Teacher	Do you think the children will want to know what Shane is playing?

Mary thinks hard, remembering her last story.

Mary	He is playing with his doll.

Now, when Mary stands up and reads her piece, children will still have questions. However, subtle messages about readers and meaning have been given to the writer.

If this process is continued throughout their first three years of schooling, children learn thousands of questioning models on which to draw. They are then in an excellent position to start asking questions of a writing partner.

In 1991 twenty Southland schools took part in a Ministry of Education writing curriculum contract. The contract was based around an Action Research model. One school collected data on Year Four children and their ability to partner conference. The results were not reassuring. They decided that only thirty per cent of these conferences were worthwhile. The reason? Children could not ask questions.

The school then observed their new entrant children. They found many who had difficulty in asking questions. Those who did question, usually asked 'Why?' It was decided that the teachers would write with their children every day. The children would be encouraged to ask questions of the teacher's writing. These questions were: who, what, when, why, which, where and how.

Initially, the new-entrant teacher would draw a picture and pin cards on the clothing of a selected group of children. They then became: Mr When, Mrs Which, Ms Why, Mr How, etc. The teacher would ask the questions, and the children would give the answers. Later in the day when children read their writing to the class, the teacher would say: 'Who has a 'what' question for Mary?' 'Who has a 'where' question?', etc.

The senior class teacher had to work in a similar way. Although she did not draw pictures or use such names as 'Mr When' to name the cards, selected children were issued with question cards. These children were expected to ask questions of their teacher's writing.

The moral of the story? Before introducing partner conferencing, make sure your children have base-line skills. Don't assume it: teach it.

It is not uncommon for junior school teachers to prepare their children for a time when they will be expected to work with a partner. Often they are required to discuss their intended topic before writing. Sometimes at the end of a session they will share their writing with a friend. This can be quite interesting, as often both children will read at the same time. Even though they might not listen to each other, they seem to enjoy this opportunity to read to an audience.

The Writing Partner

The writing partner becomes the third link in the chain. Partners are yet other audiences who question writers. The teacher cannot be everywhere at once, so as children get older they are expected to do more questioning of content. Partners can be used to set the scene before writing starts, act as sounding boards as the writing progresses, and review what has been written at the end of the session. Partner conferencing should be based around routine.

Where these conferences are successful, children know exactly what is expected of them. A class chart (such as the one shown here) is a good idea for children to use when writing.

Teachers may introduce children to partner conferencing when they consider they have the skills and abilities to learn from partner sharing. Some able Year Two children may find working with a partner rewarding. At the other end of the spectrum, some Year Five children may not have basic language and listening skills to work successfully with a partner.

The Group Conference

Every teacher knows the difficulty of trying to be all things to all people. They know they cannot be in thirty places at once. If children

---

This chart can be used to establish conferencing routines. ▼

Partner Conferences

Writer:
1. Tell your partner what the piece is about.
2. Identify any help you require.
3. Read the last paragraph (half page) to your partner.

Partner:
1. Listen carefully. Ask questions about anything you do not understand.
2. Try to give the advice requested.
3. Ask what the writer is going to do next.

Change roles.

take over much of the questioning in relation to text, the teacher can gain time to work with individuals who need frequent assistance.

By the time they have had several years' experience of working with writing partners, most children are capable of learning how to respond within a group.

Some teachers start children into group work by identifying those who are proficient at working in a paired setting. Initially, the teacher might only establish one group. Time is spent teaching the group a number of routines. They must know how these conferences will be handled. A starting point could be for the teacher to meet with the group once a week, leaving the group to have another weekly meeting by themselves.

As time goes on the teacher may want to establish a second group. The children from the first group might be split to establish two new groups.

In classes where children have had several years of group conferencing experiences, the class may be put into set groups from early in the year. It is advisable not to keep changing these groups as children need time to feel safe in confiding and sharing with others. Once again conferences are based on routine. I would suggest a chart such as the one shown here.

Children by this time should be starting to learn to be self-critical of their writing. Teachers can teach this by asking children to analyse their work.

Teacher How do you feel about this piece of writing, Jade?
Jade What do you mean?
Teacher Are you happy with it?
Jade Yes.
Teacher Can you find a section of the writing that pleases you?
Jade I like the beginning. I think I'm getting good at writing interesting beginnings.
Teacher Let me hear it.
  ... .
Teacher Is there a part of your writing that you think could be improved?
Jade No, I think it's all okay. I'm not sure about the ending yet.
Teacher What did you think you might write?

If this sort of interaction is happening between teacher and child the same language is often carried over into group conferences.

Jade I'm writing about being caught on a volcanic mountain during an eruption. I've made a start, but I'm not really happy with it and I would like the group to help.

  After others have talked to the group ...
Simon What part are you unhappy with? Is it the beginning, the middle or the end?
Jade The beginning is okay. I think it's the ending. I want a way of escaping rocks and stuff. I can't think of anything.
Tala Read it to us. We might be able to help.

> **Group Conference**
>
> 1. Each person in the group speaks. Tell the group:
>   - What your current piece is about.
>   - Where you are within the piece.
>   - If there is something you want to share or assistance you require.
> 2. When everyone has spoken, return to those children who said they wanted the group's assistance.
> 3. Work your way through the problems identified.

▲ This class chart can be used to establish conferencing routines when writing.

> Last Saterday I went to Underwater wold. I was goodfun. I got a hat and a badge. When we got home we played on the trampolin. I fell off but didn't get hert.

> Last Saterday I went to Underwater Wold. You can see the fish in the lake. You go down some steps and look in a wmdow. The fish come up to the glass. There are some big trot down there. I got a hat and a badge. It had Underwater Wold on it.

▲ These two samples show a story before (top) and after (bottom) conferencing.

The section is read; the children respond. Hopefully during these conferences the writers learn to question, think and solve problems.

Self-Conferencing

The group conferencing is one step away from self-questioning and finding independent solutions to writing problems. The purpose of these conferencing models is to demonstrate questioning and thinking so that the writer thinks and solves writing problems without having to consult a committee.

The focus is always on meaning. The children should discover how to revise by taking part in shared and guided writing experiences. They should know how to go about changing the meaning of text. Once the meaning is clear, the writer becomes the proofreader.

John Heenan's concern is that this self-conferencing does not develop because there is no continuity of method throughout most schools. If some classes question and some do not, the result is that the children learn nothing about writing, questioning and thinking. He is probably right.

Proofreading and Editing

The composition of the garden looks fine. Small shrubs break the line of the house. Taller trees and shrubs give privacy on the boundaries; the lawn looks lush and green. From a distance our property looks neat and interesting.

Sadly there comes a time when most gardeners realise that their lawns are dying. Moss has taken over; the moss must be removed. Weeds are attacking the borders; the borders must be weeded. Some of the larger shrubs are showing signs of disease; the shrubs must be pruned and sprayed. Our gardener takes responsibility for removing the moss, pulling the weeds, pruning and spraying the shrubs. This is what ownership is all about.

Many children view the teacher as the gardener. They are quite content to sow the seeds, but not all are anxious to pull the weeds.

My wife knows it is folly to set me loose in the garden. I follow a scorched earth policy. I usually pull out plants, weeds, shrubs and flowers. My wife finds it easier to confine my weeding to cabbages and other larger vegetable plants. Usually, I then manage my weeding task.

Introducing children to proofreading is like selecting weeding. Learners need to recognise aspects of their writing and to take responsibility for correcting a few things at a time. As they learn, responsibility is increased. The teacher's role is to make the task manageable. This means concentrating on what children can do, rather than focusing, as teachers have done in the past, on what they cannot.

I now believe I know why as a child I was not good at proofreading. The thought of having to correct everything was too great for me to handle. As well as that, I had teachers who were excellent gardeners.

Of course the objective of the exercise is to have children who eventually take good care of their own gardens, Realistically, some children will always see weeds in flowers and flowers in weeds. I believe children must first stand back and see the whole garden before we ask them to undertake the weeding. Writing is about conveying meaning. Spelling and punctuation make the task of reading easier, but first writers need to have something to say. So much for the Garden Show – back to the writing.

Using the *I Can* Lists

The *I Am Learning* and *I Can* list idea was originally developed by Donald Graves. It was adapted and used in *Dancing with the Pen*. This method is based on the belief that children should be responsible for what they know, and that task difficulty should be managed by the teacher. The lists are based on the following briefs:
- *Learners* are responsible for *what they know*.
- The *teacher* is responsible for *what they do not know*.
- *Both* are responsible for what the *learner is currently learning*.

The hardest task is the initial setting up of the *I Can* list. It is possible to ask older children to draw up their own list and then negotiate the final list with the child. It is surprising to find out that some children are totally unaware of what they know. Some children have little belief in themselves as learners. They often have difficulty in identifying what they know.

Having established the *I Can* list, the next thing is to identify one new learning goal. This is recorded in the *I Am Learning* list. Children should be able to talk about what they know and what they are trying to learn.

During the first term of 1994 I observed seven teachers who worked with middle- and senior-school children. The common difficulty mentioned in using this method was maintaining the lists. This is of course most difficult if you are trying to monitor thirty children at a time.

In the chapter 'Why the Fuss about Genre?', I suggested that teachers consider monitoring target groups so that they may collect data over a longer period of time. To this end I would identify a number of children each week so that each month all lists were updated. It is far easier checking eight lists a week than trying to check thirty.

It might be argued that some do not get monitored until the end of the first month. First, however, it will probably take until the end of the first month to set up all the lists. Second, any observations teachers may want to make outside the target group can still be recorded. Having a systematic method is designed to make sure all children have data collected about their progress and that the collection process is going to be manageable for the teacher.

Once these lists are established, children are expected to self-correct everything on their *I Can* list. They are also expected to make an effort to correct what has been recorded on their *I Am Learning* list. Proofreading can be handled thus.

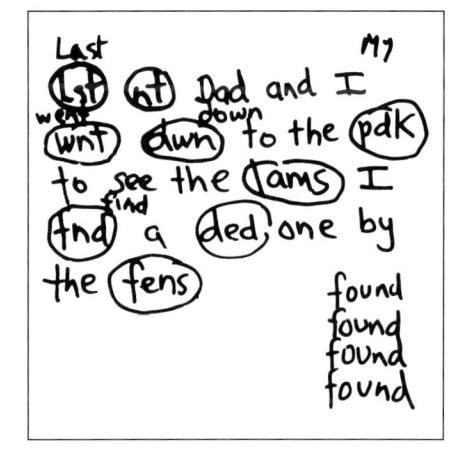

▲ A sample showing a child's self-correction at age 6 years.

▲ These two samples show different types of spellers. The top sample shows a phonetic speller, while the bottom sample is of a visual speller.

A Model for Proofreading

1. Children write. They do not rub out, but line out.

2. They are encouraged to re-read and do a minor proofreading at the end of each session.

3. The child decides to publish. This final proofreading is done in pen, in red ink or any other colour. All children use the same coloured pen for final checking.

4. The child is responsible for finding indicated (underlined?) spelling errors. These are written above the error. They proofread everything on their *I Can* list and attempt to correct the item on the *I Am Learning* list.

5. Teacher takes work home and does a final edit. First the lists are checked and the proofreading task is evaluated. Teacher then edits in same medium as the child's original writing. What stands out on the page is the child's self-correcting, not the teacher's marking.

6. A brief post-editing conference is held. The child's work, proof-reading and learning item are discussed. A decision is made about publication.

Spelling

Children need to be encouraged into doing some self-correction of spelling. When the child has reached the phonetic stage of spelling development, the child should be encouraged to attempt to find words that are visually close to correct.

The phonetic speller has achieved complete sound sequencing of dominant sounds within words.

The following are some common spelling attempts: wnt = went, lst = last, ppl = people, brk = break, ddt = didn't, hd = had. Most children will locate these words from an alphabetical list as they can visually recognise the word.

In the past children have been encouraged to use word lists to find and copy words. They know want starts with a 'w' but when they turn to the 'w' list there are sixty words that start with 'w'. They often end up totally confused. (See pp. 60–66 *Dancing with the Pen*, Learning Media, 1991.)

Texts on developmental spelling are *Spel is a Four-Letter Word*, Richard Gentry (Ashton Scholastic Bright Ideas Series), and *Reading the Writing on the Wall*, Tom Nicholson (Dunmore Press).

Alphabetical lists

My 1994 observations of new-entrant writers conclusively proved that alphabetical word lists are only useful when children have a visual impression of a word. I observed a child looking for the word church. Her first attempt was to look in the 't' list (she called it a 'turch'). Another child told her it started with a 'c'. She then spent fifteen minutes looking up and down both the 't' and 'c' lists and never found the word. If she could have made an attempt and got as close as 'ch', she might have had some chance of success.

In my travels I have found some excellent spelling proofreading from quite young children. The Year Two children at Peterhead School in Hastings were very able proofreaders. They had an area of the classroom set up as a correcting centre and they took the correcting of spelling as a normal part of their writing. These children had established a good habit that must be maintained, not a bad habit to break.

How many times have teachers said to children, 'You are in the senior school; you must now learn to check your spelling.' I know five-year-old children who are ready to check their own spelling, and some Year Four children who are not. It is stage, not age, that is important.

It is suggested that incorrectly spelled words be checked and recorded in a notebook, and that children be challenged to learn them; you would be surprised how many take up the challenge.

In the past, slower children have been given their ten words a week to remember the order of four to five letters for each of the ten words, without having any visual memory. I would liken it to adults being asked to remember ten random phone numbers in case 'you might want to ring them up one day.'

The teacher editor

In the past many teachers thought of conferencing as being the time when child and teacher go through the child's writing; the teacher pointing out all the mistakes, and the child remembering not to make them the next time.

Marie Clay wrote in *What Did I Write* (Heinemann, 1977) that this is a total waste of time. 'By the time the teacher talks about the fourth error, the child has forgotten the first.'

If the school policy is one that stipulates that children have to take responsibility for their own proofreading, and all keep to the policy, standards will improve.

Publication

At one time I thought that it was vital that learner writers publish their own writing. I have changed my mind.

Why do writers publish? The reason of course, is to enable people to read their work. Many children lack coordination, make transposing mistakes and when finished, their work looks no different from the original draft. These children are not stupid. They know others are not going to read their work. In many cases, although they might have reasonable ideas and information, it is too hard to read.

For these children teachers must look for other methods of publishing:
- Parent helpers with type skills, both in class and at home.
- Teacher typing, although often time is against this option.
- Using other children to assist.
- Publishing by reading onto tape, sometimes using the teacher's voice to make it sound more interesting.

Some Key Conclusions

Meaning always comes first. Teachers must try to avoid negative teaching.

Conferencing methods such as class, partner, group and teacher conferences are based on work routine. They are important in providing questioning models that lead the writer to self-conferencing.

The writers take responsibility for what they know. *I Can* and *I Am Learning* lists make this possible.

The teacher is the final editor. Work that is to be published must be correct.

Children start proofreading, and learning spelling from the time they are phonetic spellers. It is stage, not age, that is important.

Sometimes less able children, and able children who write longer pieces, need outside help with publication.

- More visual publications, lots of illustration with some clearly written text.

The able child who has written a longer than normal piece may also need this type of publishing assistance.

My 1994 research showed that children enjoy publication. It came out very clearly when children were asked what they had enjoyed about writing during the period of the research. We also know that when children are given time to produce a quality product they are keen to write something new.

It has been said that a quality process should deliver a quality product. If children do not experience the success and satisfaction of turning out a piece of writing, in which they can feel some pride, the school writing programme is failing to deliver to its students.

6

In this chapter

- The National Educational Monitoring Project
- Invented spelling

The Vexing Question of Spelling

Of late, as I travel the country delivering my seminars, my courses dealing with spelling seem to be drawing the most participants. Everyone knows that spelling is important, but schools seem unsure as to exactly what they should be doing in order that their children become successful in this basic skill of writing.

I jokingly tell the teachers that they should be thankful that there is not a spelling curriculum, otherwise there would be eight levels of achievement and schools would be expected to monitor children against a range of learning outcomes. While everyone is thoroughly sick of new curriculums, exactly what to do about spelling is not clearly defined within the current curriculum.

Of course, it is there. It is part of exploring language, and therefore must be handled within the various processes of writing. It is also a basic skill of writing. If students can't spell, they can't write. It's that simple.

When I was at school in the 1950s we had subjects called Reading, Handwriting, Spelling and Composition. Each one had its own slot on the timetable, and all were treated as separate subjects. Spelling was treated a bit like a quiz show – it might as well have been *Mastermind* as far as I was concerned. Every week we were given twenty-five words to learn in order to pass the dreaded Friday inquisition. On many occasions my mother sent me to bed in tears in response to her strenuous efforts to prepare me for the Friday ordeal. Usually I managed to pass these Friday tests. I always managed to achieve *Very Good* or *Excellent* on my report cards, yet I was never a natural speller. If they had ever re-tested me sometime during the following week, I would have been lucky to have scored ten.

Ten was an important number. In one of my classes, if you scored less than ten, you got the strap. Several boys in my class got the belt every week. It did not seem to improve their spelling. The name of the game seemed to be that you learned how to spell the words so that one day – when you needed to – you would be able to write them. We never saw any link between Spelling and Composition.

This two-weekly session of writing called Composition generated many errors. Teachers 'red-lined' every mistake they could find. We looked at the marks and then forgot all about them. I really believed that I was keeping my teacher in work; I am sure teachers believed this to be one of their key responsibilities. Both teacher and pupil played their part to the full.

When I started teaching, I operated in much the same way. The programme of the early 1970s was Arvidson. This system was built on word frequency, and children tried to work their way through a series of levels. Every month I religiously undertook the task of giving all my children a levels test. Some children never got off Level 1. I remember miscounting one boy's score so that he could finally move on to Level 2. If I hadn't been so considerate, I believe he would have finished secondary school on Level 1. Once again, there was no correlation between 'real' writing and spelling. We did word study based on their level lists, but there was no cross-over into the writing programme.

The 1963 syllabus had a quote that was years ahead of its time:

Spelling is a tool of written expression and not an end in itself.

This quote could sum up the current view of spelling and how I believe it should be applied to the current curriculum.

The National Educational Monitoring Project

As mentioned earlier in this text, the NEMP tests of 1999 stated that 'spelling and punctuation show need for improvement'. This was our committee being evasive. We could have said, 'overall, spelling standards were poor,' but, imagine what a field-day the media would have had with that!

The same thing could be said of handwriting standards. There were only two levels mentioned in the report. Average and above average. In my opinion the examples given at these levels were quite poor. Thank goodness we didn't publish some of the below-average samples!

The project found that children were unable to identify errors and that self-correction was poor. *We stipulated the need for schools to develop common methods of error identification that would be used across all class levels.* One of my pet theories is that children must learn to identify probable errors at the time of writing, not wait until they have written before going back to locate errors. Over the last twenty years I have observed thousands of children engaging in proofreading their writing. Very few children are able spot their mistakes. I believe that with the passage of time, the eye tricks the brain into thinking the word is right. There is so much text that the child becomes 'print blind'.

Earlier in this text, I have suggested the underlining of probable errors from the time the child becomes a phonetic speller. These words should be self-corrected and should form the basis of learning lists. By the time children reach middle-school age, the underlining should be a mark less than a centimeter long; just enough to draw the eye to the possibility that the word *might* be incorrect. If this is not maintained throughout the school, I believe schools will *never* improve spelling self-correction.

Invented spelling

Earlier in this text *invented* or *approximated* spelling has been discussed. I am not going back over this. However, there are some things that we must address.

First, invented spelling should be viewed as a developmental process. That means that children should pass through a range of stages on their way to correct spelling. This could be viewed in the same way a child moves from rolling, to crawling, to walking. If I had a child still crawling at the age of nine, I would be really worried. Yet, in spelling terms we still have 'crawlers' at the age of twelve or thirteen. They are not getting any better.

Recently while I was in a school working with some Year Four and Five children, one girl was trying to spell *said*. She tried: *sead*, *saed* and *seed*. Many children in this room were having problems with words such as: *they* (thay), *there* (ther), *had* (hat), and a range of other quite simple, basic words. These children are in trouble, and there are thousands of others throughout the country.

I believe we must be more proactive in developing a core of known words from an early age, and expect that children of the age of nine and ten will be leaving 'invented spelling' behind them.

Reasons Why We Need to Address Spelling

On my courses, I first ask teachers to identify the reasons we need spelling programmes. Usually the following are discussed:
- Sound spelling helps the child write with speed and ease, thus allowing the writer to concentrate on the ideas to be expressed.
- Correct spelling leads to easier interpretation by the reader.
- It develops a feeling of self-assurance, confidence and independence.
- It is a vocational and social skill which is rightly or wrongly used by society to judge literacy.

It is interesting to find that these same elements were identified by a group of teachers working on the Southland District Inspector of Schools Spelling Committee (1970). Basic learning skills never change.

We then discuss the aims of a sound school spelling programme. The following points usually emerge:
- to be able to spell easily and accurately the words required for written language
- to teach an efficient method of checking spelling
- to stimulate the children's interest in the English language with a view to extending their vocabulary
- to equip the child with an efficient method of learning to spell a word
- to develop a spelling conscience.

Let's explore each of these aims.

To be able to spell easily and accurately the words required for written language
I have mentioned earlier in this text that it is important that children have a good written sight vocabulary. By the end of Year One children should

have achieved a number of learning objectives. These might include:
- an ability to write about twenty-five to thirty sight words accurately
- a knowledge of the alphabet
- an ability to link a number of letter sounds to letter names
- be able to make approximations of interest words using an inventive spelling system.

These twenty-five to thirty words closely equate to the words teachers want children to learn during *Emergent* reading instruction. If they are reading and writing these words regularly, mastery will be achieved quite naturally. This is fully covered in the chapter *Emerging as a Writer*.

Good writers do not invent everything. A close inspection of the writing sample on page 73 shows that the child wrote 54 words. There were 14 errors. This makes for an accuracy rate of around 75 per cent. Most children who are good 'inventors' also have a large lexicon of known high-frequency words. Percentage accuracy should increase with maturity. The missing factor with this sample is that there is no indication of probable errors and no self-correction.

Donald Graves states in his latest book *A Fresh Look at Writing* that children by Grade 1 need to know about thirty words. By Grade 3 – about eight years of age – they should have a bank of about 100 known words. He uses the *Fry 100 Common Words* which he includes in his book. He states that these words equate to about 75 per cent of all written language. This list seems to bear a strong similarity to the *Essential Lists* of *Spell Write*. This brings us to the second aim:

To teach an efficient method of checking spelling

As already stated, I have always been a strong advocate of underlining possible errors at the time of writing. I have included an example on p. 73 from a seven-year-old who has been taught this method and is starting to make some self-corrections. These words will be transferred to her learning list at the start of each week.

This method follows right through this particular school. It is introduced when children reach the *phonetic* stage of spelling development, i.e. they are making close approximations, e.g. lst (last), ppel (people), brk (break), frst (forest).

These attempts are so close that the child should be able to use a word resource to self-correct them.

I mentioned my own early experiences with spelling learning lists. I may have given the impression I am totally against them, but this is not the case. The words I had to learn were all strangers. This child has at least a nodding acquaintance with the above words. They are words the child is trying to write, and they are only a letter or two out. These words could also be termed *high frequency*, and therefore the learner needs to know how to spell them.

To stimulate the children's interest in the English language with a view to extending their vocabulary

If children are not making enough errors to maintain a learning list there are two remedies.
1. Use a published mastery list to supplement child error.

2. Introduce them to new language that they will then be tempted to use.

Mastery lists

I have already mentioned *Spell Write*. Another list that is used extensively in New Zealand schools is Peter De Ath's *You Can Spell* (Longman Paul, 1993). While not an advocate of all the workbooks that go along with the lists, I think the mastery lists provided might make a useful supplementary list.

Every Monday morning the child featured in the previous example of self-correction transfers her weekly errors to a learning list. If she has ten errors to learn, that is deemed to be sufficient. If she has gaps, she is tested on one of the De Ath mastery list sheets. Each child has a list at their level of competency. Her partner will take her down the list until she has filled the gaps. This book then is taken home and the parents conduct nightly tests. Any word still not known by the week's end is transferred to the next week's column. The parent then signs off the list.

Every Friday morning the teacher makes a quick circuit of the room checking signatures. If they are not signed off, the teacher might do a one-to-one test, or have another pupil conduct a spot test. Mostly, however, these lists are checked off by parents. There is no need for a Friday test. Why test words that have already been tested?

Vocabulary extension

I mentioned earlier that the NEMP test results showed that children did not have an adequate supply of vivid language to write interesting descriptions. I believe that a major part of any English programme must be language extension. This comes into the *Exploring Language* process of the curriculum.

In the 1970s our school used a programme called *Sounds of Language* by Bill Martin Jr. This *alternative language* programme required the children and teacher to cooperatively write wall stories. Adjectives were identified and alternative words were listed below each adjective. Different colours were used so that different versions of the text could be read. Children were encouraged to use the thesaurus to look for alternatives; then the story was read back in its various forms. 'Let's read the "red" version; let's read the "blue" version.'

This is, of course, a type of *shared writing*. I have used the same techniques in getting the children to help me with the pirate story on page 84 (boat/ship/vessel). I believe that there needs to be a lot more language extension if we are going to develop better writers. At the same time, teachers will be developing new words that children will eventually learn. A key spelling skill must be learning how to use a thesaurus (see p. 76 example) and how to improve the overall quality of the writing.

Exploring language

This takes place within the reading programme. First look for good examples of descriptive text. Then identify the adjectives, look for the examples of metaphor and simile or examples of imagery. Children need to study how these techniques are used by professional writers.

'Newsboard' provides junior school children an opportunity to explore language and develop a knowledge of a variety of spelling rules. 'Newsboard' could be termed a junior spelling programme. Teachers should be encouraging children to look for:

Patterns within words:
Some examples are cat, mat, pat, and, sand, hand, make, take, wake. Word generation is a key spelling ability.

Rules for adding endings:
- Words ending in silent letter
- Short vowel words
- Long vowel words
- Words ending in y.

Punctuation:
- Writing in sentences
- Speech marks
- Comma
- Question mark
- Exclamation mark.

Contracted words and compound words:
All of the above and any related skills can be developed through 'Newsboard'.

Many of these elements can be taught during reading, or current events. I doubt that teachers can find yet another twenty minutes on an already crowded timetable for a specific time called *Spelling*. It must be integrated.

* Richard Gentry identifies specific rules to be taught in his book *Spel is a Four Letter Word* (Ashton Scholastic)

Senior-school children

Using the *dictionary* and *thesaurus*.
Word derivations:

aqua water	**audio** I hear	**capio** I take	**centum** a hundred
calmo I shout	**creo** I create	**curro** I run	**decem** ten
dico I say	**duco** I lead	**facio** I make	**finis** an end
fortis strong	**home** a man	**impero** I command	**liber** free
malus bad	**manus** hand	**nitto** I send	**navis** a ship
octo eight	**pello** I drive	**pendeo** I hang	**ped** foot
planus level	**plus** more	**porto** I carry	**poto** drink
primus first	**pro** before	**rego** I rule	**rota** a wheel
ruptus broken	**scribe** I write	**specio** I see	**teneo** I hold
vidoe I see	**vinco** I overcome	**volvo** I roll	**amo** I love
bellum war	**bene** good	**caput** head	**civis** citizen

Generalisations and Conventions:
- Capital letters. Proper nouns and at start of sentence.
- Apostrophe of possession
- Personal pronouns not requiring the apostrophe of possession.
- Plural forms that change in form (woman/women)
- Adding a suffix to a word ending in 'e' (make/making)
- Adding a suffix to a word ending in 'y' (baby/babies)
- Adding a prefix to build a word.
- Adding a suffix to a word of one syllable or accented on the last syllable (run/running begin/beginning).
- The letter 'q' is followed by a 'u'.

To equip the child with an efficient method of learning to spell a word

Children and parents must be taught how to learn spelling words. I believe the best method is probably: *Look, cover, write, check. Look, cover, write, check.*

When I was young, my mother said a word and I had to spell it. I did not have a good auditory memory, and thus it became a frustrating memory test. I believe that I would probably have done better if I had been asked to write the words down. I am a far better visual learner and would have possibly gained mastery quicker using this method.

Some children have excellent visual memory. They see a word once and they never forget it. Lesser mortals often have problems retaining even simple words. The 'good' spellers often lose patience with the 'dead heads'. I find it quite interesting that the ones who heavily emphasise spelling are the ones who find it easy.

To develop a spelling conscience

This is so easy to say but harder to do. The NEMP interviewed the Year Four and Year Eight children that were part of the 1999 survey. The majority identified the teacher as being their major reader. While this is the case they will never develop a spelling conscience.

One of the major factors of *Expressive Writing* is that reader and writer know each other so well that they expect their 'friends' to cut them some slack when it comes to spelling. Many children equate teacher with mum, dad or big brother or sister. They expect that their teachers 'love' them and will not be too annoyed about poor spelling.

On the other hand, there are children who think it is the teacher's role to find all their spelling errors, i.e. make sure that their work is correct before it is passed on to the reader. In both instances, the child does not accept responsibility for his or her writing. Children will only start developing a spelling conscience if:
- there is a real reader going to read their work
- they do not know the reader
- they are expected to take responsibility for their own writing
- publication is part of the overall process.

So what of 'Spelling Time' on the classroom timetable?

Donald Graves states:

> The traditional week-long spelling learning lists found in publishers' books with Monday and Friday tests has a bleak history.

He goes on to quote research done by Cohen that shows that calling attention to parts, phonetic re-spellings and dictionary skills can actually regress children's spelling ability. Cohen states that spelling books are useful for their word lists.

Gentry, on the other hand, says that senior children need about fifteen minutes each day on word study.

If teachers believe this, I don't think this fifteen minutes should be timetabled. As already mentioned, the curriculum is already so overcrowded that finding extra time is not easy.

What does happen when teachers allocate this time is that real writing disappears! Earlier this year I happened to be visiting one of my final-year students. I expected to see her teaching, but instead I was subjected to watching her oversee book work. I became quite bored, so I called over a bright-eyed young girl to find out what she was doing.

Hood	What are you up to?
Niki	We're finding all the verbs.
Hood	Why?
Niki	Don't ask me.
Hood	Where's your writing book?
Niki	My handwriting book?
Hood	No, the one you do your stories in.
	Niki retreated and returned with a book.
Nicki	This is my language book.
	It was April. She had completed two pieces of writing. The first was a recount of going to Wellington during the holidays. Second was a set of instructions on how to make a painting shirt.
Hood	Where are your stories?
Nicki	I'm in the big kids' room now. We don't write stories.
	I laughingly approached the teacher.
Hood	The little girl over there tells me she is in the big kids' room and that they don't write stories.
Teacher	They'll be writing narratives next term.

Her logic was that if they studied 'verbs' they would write better instructions. If they studied 'adjectives' they would write better narratives. Therefore they did exercises or completed worksheets every day, but only wrote two pieces in ten weeks. I can't see much logic in that.

Teachers must look for opportunities to study language in context. As already mentioned, it is important that they know about verbs, adjectives, nouns, adverbs, etc. But it is *how* this knowledge is imparted that is important. There is a strong body of research that states that this is best done within the context of *real* writing so that children get an opportunity to use what they have discovered.

This chapter deals with some of the issues about spelling. Spelling will be a subject of debate as long are there are teachers, parents and pupils who find difficulty with spelling. I hope by identifying some areas of concern, schools can start deciding how to handle this vexing matter.

Some Key Conclusions

Children need to be able to spell in order to write.

Spelling is a developmental process.

Children need to learn to self-correct.

Common school policy is essential.

Spelling is part of the 'explaining language' process

Word study/'Newsboard' approaches teach spelling patterns.

Involved spelling should lead to accurate spelling.

Teach spelling rules that work all the time.

7

In this chapter

- The philosophy and effects of curriculum change
- The New Zealand English Curriculum
- The writing strand
- Problems
- Assessment and understanding

Working with the English Curriculum

Throughout the Western world the last ten years has seen rapid curriculum change. Many involved in education would argue that these changes have been rushed and at times ill considered. There is no question that these changes have found schools having to rethink their delivery and teaching of the curriculum.

The winds of change grew out of Margaret Thatcher's England and were inspired by a drive for what the political masters called 'accountability'. Schools and their teachers were expected to be accountable to their parent community, while at the same time facing outside pressure to conform to regulations set in place by the governing body.

The Philosophy and Effects of Curriculum Change

A major factor in this time of change has been a new philosophy of educational resourcing. This has had an impact on how schools are governed. The new 'hands off' philosophy has become the foundation of the 'self-managing' school. It has also, in my opinion, seen the demise of educational leadership from the various agencies of central government. While the administration continues to regulate curriculum, it has passed responsibility for working out how these changes might be delivered into the hands of individual schools.

Throughout the Western world, contracted educators have been required to implement a range of new curriculum statements. In England, parts of Canada, New Zealand and Australia teachers have had to assimilate an ever-growing mountain of material. In the case of New Zealand, the recent English curriculum was written by one group, responded to in draft form, and then revised by a second writing group. The production of this document had to be achieved within a very tight time-frame.

The New Zealand education system has also been influenced by a philosophy of rapid change. Change is a great idea if you are not the one being asked to make the change. Sadly, the pressures placed on schools, teachers and a small number of teacher support staff have resulted in many dedicated people leaving the profession.

The New Zealand experience

In 1990 our team of writers wrote *Dancing with the Pen*, the official handbook on the teaching of writing. We were never asked to contribute to how the writing strand of the new curriculum should be developed. Thus, the people who constructed the teacher philosophy, were never part of writing the content. This type of curriculum development would never – and could never – have been countenanced under the previous administration.

There was a time when new developments had to be well tested and amended under classroom conditions before being introduced to schools. Change was always supported by well trained staff who led programmes of professional development. In the climate of *Today's Schools* the number of new curriculum statements being introduced, the number of teachers needing to be trained and the speed of change, have made a rational system of curriculum introduction very difficult.

It is common knowledge that in England curriculum documents have had to be revised and changed several times since their introduction. As in New Zealand, these statements were produced quickly, then passed into the system for implementation. Teachers found many shortcomings in these documents, and after a short period of time some revision was required. Speed, as on the road, has its price.

I am sure that teachers would not argue against the philosophy of curriculum review. There is no argument that in New Zealand the English curriculum was in need of revision, and that there have been some positive refinements outlined in the current document. My argument is with the manner in which these documents have been written, and the frequency of the introduction of new curriculum statements into the school system. The pace of change, in my opinion, has been too great.

The New Zealand English Curriculum

The New Zealand English Curriculum outlines three strands of language:
- Oral Language
- Written Language (includes Reading and Writing)
- Visual Language.

The Australian document has followed this same pattern, so once again we see evidence of this flow-on effect moving from system to system throughout the Western world.

This document has been fairly well received by teachers. Its strength is that it endeavours to set out learning progression over eight levels of achievement. It has the worthwhile philosophy of providing learner-centred educational outcomes rather than basing outcomes on class or age. It has tried to keep faith with the New Zealand concept of *whole langauge* learning, where language is learned in context through a variety of approaches. The writers were instructed to keep to the philosophies first established in the national reading handbook *Reading in Junior Classes* and the writing handbook *Dancing with the Pen*. It could be said that the various writing teams tried their best to do the impossible – and almost succeeded.

The writers' task, set by the Ministry of Education, was a difficult one. Initial problems were faced as to how to marry a behaviourist belief structure into a document that would ask teachers to assess children against consumerist outcomes. The document eventually ended up with a behaviourist philosophy, followed by a set of knowledge-based objectives. Internationally respected educational researcher Dr Warwick Elley argued that language could not be learned sequentially. He pointed out that what one child might find complex, another might find simple. What a teacher imagined would cause difficulty, a number of children might find easy.

Curriculum objectives

The original writers tried their best to get over these problems by broad-banking curriculum objectives through a number of levels. This did not suit the political direction set within the system of curriculum review. Important people had been determined that curriculum statements would be divided into eight levels, each level having an achievement objective. The Ministry of Education then contracted a second team of writers to review the draft statement. While achieving the desired outcome, the final set of objectives was very wordy and open to wide interpretation. To give an example:

- A Level 1 objective: (Children aged five to seven)
  Recount experiences in authentic contexts.
- A Level 2 objective: (Children aged six to nine)
  Recount events in a range of authentic contexts.

Both are contexts – *plural*. What does the word 'range' add to the meaning of the objective? Look at another example.
Levels 1, 2, 3 and 4 states:
Children can write instructions.
When teachers read Level 5 they find it now states:
Write coherent, logical instruction.

I would argue that if the instructions at Level 1 are not 'logical and coherent', they are *not* instructions. There must be different criteria required to judge the progress of these children.

The problem with most of these curriculum statements is that teachers cannot teach from them. They are full of verbiage and sadly, schools must make their own interpretations as to what the curriculum is asking them to teach. This, of course, is the philosophy of the self-managing school. But is it cost-efficient?

Learning outcomes

Another problem also arises from this approach. Until learning outcomes are identified, there is *nothing* to measure. Throughout New Zealand, many schools are spending hours and hours trying to identify what they are required to teach. Most would agree that the in-service training provided has been inadequate. Many teachers are unaware of the learning progression they should be developing and what is developmentally appropriate to different age groups.

One Dunedin teacher, struggling with a particularly difficult class of new entrants, complained to me that the curriculum was worthless. 'How can I teach them this?' she stated pointing to the Level 1 objective: *Can write instructions and recount events in authentic contexts.* The teacher was bemused, 'They will be lucky if they can do this after three years ... where is Level Zero!'

Looking at her children, I could see her problem, but then it suddenly occurred to me that the teacher thought she was expected to teach the curriculum objectives. I had to explain that she had to set achievable learning outcomes in order that eventually they could achieve at Level 1. The achievements objectives are not a ladder to be climbed; more of a zig zag. Each step being identified by a learning objective. Her response? 'What good is a curriculum that does not tell me what I am to teach!'

I had one teacher ask me why her children were unable to complete the principal's writing assessment task. The task for these six- and seven-year-old children was to write a third-person recount. Only three children out of thirty managed to complete this task. While this surprised the principal, it did not surprise me. The task was developmentally inappropriate. Children of this age are so egocentric that thinking and writing in the third person is quite difficult, and for most, impossible.

As the writers of *Dancing with the Pen*, I feel we might have been asked to tie the learning outcomes to the philosophy set out in the handbook to the curriculum. I do not believe this has really been achieved. Each group viewed the problem from a different perspective. The first group of writers could not fully grasp our intention, so they produced their own vision. The second group produced theirs. I am not saying one group is right or the other wrong. Each view is different, and I believe slightly out-of-step with the one we tried to promote in the handbook.

While working with a group of teachers in Auckland, I was asked why I hadn't written something to assist teachers in interpreting the expectations of the English Curriculum. I told them it was too difficult, and I was leaving it to the schools. This was, of course, partly a joke, but now I have attempted to put something down on paper I have found it a most daunting task. In this new edition of *Left to Write Too* I have made an attempt to look at the writing strand of the national curriculum, Levels 1–4 (children aged five to thirteen).

▲ This piece of expressive writing was done by a six-year-old.

The Writing Strand

There seems to be a common belief that there are three types of writing that children need to be able to control:
- Expressive writing
- Poetic writing
- Transactional writing.

For the sake of expediency, let's look at some simplistic definitions of these sub-divisions.

Expressive writing

This is writing of the self. Often writer and reader are the same person. If not, they are so close that there is a range of shared understandings

> The children stood on the cliff. Below them in the harbour they saw a boat. It was an old boat, square rigged with 2 masts. Her orange sails which were once bright and gay were patched, faded, ragged and hung limply. Her gilded dragon's-head on the bow was chipped and there was not much paint left on her. What there was was flaking. She tilted slightly to port (left) and she bumped the dock in the swell. The roof had been torn off her cabin. She looked a wreck.
> The 3 children scrambled down the cliff. When they reached the dock, they ran along the wooden planks until they reached the post where the boat was moored. There was a nice looking man on the deck but he looked tired. His red cloak was stained and the end of it was frayed. It looked as if something had had it in it's mouth. His black hair was tousled and his trouser legs ragged.
> "Hello," one of the children called.
> "Hi" the man replied.

▲ This piece of poetic writing was developed by a Year Seven pupil through shared writing.

that reader and writer bring to the reading of the text. These writings are often associated with journals, logs, diaries, notes to immediate family, letters to pen-friends, shopping lists and memos.

These writings usually are left in their original state. They are not processed to the same degree as other pieces of writing. Spelling and punctuation are given cursory attention. Who proofreads their diary? Best friends remain our best friends because they accept us for what we are. They seldom write back with lists of spelling errors. That is why they are our best friends.

Poetic writing

Essentially this is the storytelling form of writing. It is crafted, planned, structured, revised and reworked. It is designed for a distant reader – someone the writer probably does not know. The writer has to be very clear with what they say. It is adjective-rich in that it requires the writer to write descriptively – setting scenes, describing characters and moulding the story together. It requires a knowledge of narrative structure and is helped by experience in reading a variety of narrative texts. Children who are keen readers usually do better poetic wriitng as they have many models to draw from. Children who are less able readers are more likely to write off events, use fewer adjectives, and find this type of writing quite difficult.

Transactional writing

This form of writing gets its name from the term 'transact' or 'pass across'. In this case the transactions are information. These writing forms are used mainly in the study of other curriculums like science, health, social studies or wherever children are required to record what they have discovered in their learning. Often children who find poetic writing difficult enjoy working transactionally because they write quite factually and have to use very few adjectives to achieve their purpose.

Problems

There are problems in putting all this in place. One problem is that nothing is purely expressive or poetic or transactional. Writing has a habit of jumping fences, making it difficult to control.

Let us look at Amy's letter to her father on the next page. Is it expressive, transactional or poetic?

I believe it is expressive/transactional. It is aimed at a very narrow audience (her father), and there are shared understandings that both Amy and her father comprehend. As we are not part of the writer's defined audience, we are not expected to understand all of the content of the letter. (Soapy is a guinea pig, Ripley is a rabbit.) At the same time it is transactional in that it passes on information. To further confuse things, it is a letter/argument. This eight-year-old has made many decisions in writing this piece. First, she decided to write rather than communicate orally with her father. Oral language was not meeting her communication need. Having made this decision, she had to decide content, genre, information, and make language choices.

If I am to assess Amy against curriculum goals, she meets most of the criteria of transactional writing at Level 5:

> ... *express and argue a point of view, linking main and supporting ideas and structuring material in an appropriate style.*

But is Amy a Level 5 writer? I doubt it. I would expect that children working at this level would not only be able to write the piece, but also be able to *explain* their choices, and how they went about writing the text. Teachers therefore have to look at more than outcomes. They also have to judge strategies and the meta-language the child has developed. A true Level 5 writer would have the flexibility to use writing in a variety of contexts.

So why did Amy write so well? It came down to having a *real* purpose and a *real* audience, which resulted in *real* writing. From my observations, I would contend that much of the writing that occurs in schools has little meaning for the pupil. Donald Graves stated that in every class of thirty children there were probably only three children working on what he called 'hot stuff' – the rest, he said, were just 'putting in their time'.

Trying to keep writing in a pure form is impossible. There are so many cross-overs that trying to monitor the writing against a narrow range of behaviours is impossible.

One young Auckland teacher had it worked out when she said, 'I now get the children to think of *audience* and *purpose*; the rest takes care of itself.' This is probably very sound advice. Teachers often look for activity that will develop a particular form of writing, but audience and purpose are often neglected. Instead of purpose and audience driving writing, there is a real danger that writing will be driven by the artificial demands made by curriculum statements. Writing instruction ends as a series of boxes, each box taken out perhaps once a term.

One major problem is that the majority (some 55 per cent of

> Dear Dad
>
> I feel very disappointed and sad Richi and I realy want a dog to have as a pet. A dog can be trained not to dig up the garden – cats can't. Dogs can come with me walking to keep me safe – usually people with dogs don't get attacked. Do you want me to get attacked? I have no sisters or brothers around my age to play with, and I get lonely. A dog could be my friend and play with me. Soapie and Ripley don't play with me, all the playing is by me. I have $600 in my bank that would pay for food and stuff for our dog for ages.
>
> P.S. I will give you time to think about it.
>
> Your lonely daughter
> AMY
>
> (Amy - Age 8.01)

children interviewed in my 1995 survey of nine- to eleven-year-old children) identify their teacher as their main reader. With expressive and poetic forms this is a not a problem because children believe the writing is fresh and original. At the same time they will not explain what they believe the teacher already knows. Take this example: 'John is coming to play.'

While I, the stranger, may want to know 'Who is John?' the teacher and children know John is the writer's best friend. There is no reason to explain. Children also think this way during narrative writing. 'It was a witch.' If you ask 'What did she look like?' you will get back 'Like a witch. You know …'. Writers never take time to explain what they think is obvious to the reader. Now, let us carry this across to transactional writing.

Children are not keen to write information that they think the teacher already knows. If a teacher takes them to a swamp and tells them about bullfrogs, children who identify the teacher as their reader rightly wonder, 'Why should I write something the teacher already knows?' There is little reason to 'revise' because they leave out the detail that they think the teacher already understands. When they write for an unknown reader, there is a need to be explicit and give the reader as much information as possible.

If senior school children are keeping a daily diary, writing to entertain, and writing to inform across the curriculum, the classroom programme is likely to provide balance. In trying to achieve this balance there are two questions of concern:
1. Do children have the strategies to gather, order, and use information?
2. Do the children know how to write in the required genre?

If the answers are in the affirmative, the programme takes care of itself. If the answers are in the negative, there is a need for teaching and support within the classroom programme.

Assessment and Understanding

In Chapter 3, 'Why the Fuss about Genre?', I have gone into some detail why schools need to have clear direction as to what they are teaching. I also made the remark that teachers cannot teach what they do not know. The same is true of assessment. If teachers do not know the different writing forms, quality assessment is impossible.

Last year I had an interesting experience while out watching one of my final-year students. Mary had her children gathered in front of her and was setting up the morning's work. The children had been engaged on a science project investigating insects. Each child had selected an insect and gathered information. It was now time to use the information.

'Right,' said Mary. 'You all have your information about your insect?'

'Yes,' replied the class.

'Great. Today I want you to write about your insect. Remember it has to have a beginning, a middle and an end.'

Most of the children got up and headed off to make a start. Some stayed behind because they wanted to question the teacher. Most teachers would not find this unusual, but one boy, David, reacted quite differently.

'This is *boring*. Why do I have to do this boring stuff?'

The teacher was quite firm. 'David, I've told you what to do. Go back to your desk and get on with it!'

'But I don't want to ...,' David started to reply.

'I've told you what to do, David, no arguing!' Mary was not going to have this lesson disrupted. She knew I was sitting there, pen poised, watching and waiting to see how she handled the situation.

David went back to his desk, still complaining loudly. While Mary had moved to another part of the room and was now trying her best to ignore him. David opened his desk, took out his books, and let the lid drop. CRASH! Every teacher and child knows that something like that is really hard to ignore.

'David, I told you to get on with our work .... QUIETLY.'

'But I don't ...'.

'NO arguing. Get to WORK! NOW!'

Mary was taking no prisoners. David opened his book, picked up a pen, and turned to his neighbour. I don't know what the neighbour said, but I know he got slashed across the ear with the pen for his trouble. The boy let out a great yell!

Mary could not let this go on. She went over and moved David's desk off into a corner.

'NOW ... get on with your work,' she demanded. It was just as well that she couldn't see the look David gave her as she headed back across the room.

While being an interested observer, I could not stand aside any longer. Mary's lesson was falling apart, so I decided to try to help her. I quietly went over to David. A transcript of our conversation went like this:

Hood	What's the problem?
David	I have to do this *boring* stuff.
Hood	What is it?
David	I have to write about this insect.
Hood	What insect is that?
David	It's a praying mantis.
Hood	How are you going to do it?
David	I don't know. *She* says it has to have a beginning, a middle and an end.
Hood	Well, tell me, what is a praying mantis?
David	It's an insect.
Hood	And ...
David	It hunts other insects.
Hood	Why is it called a praying mantis?
David	Oh, its got these funny feelers at the front and it looks as if it is praying.
Hood	That's your beginning.
David	Is it?
Hood	Yes. Tell me again. A praying mantis is ...
David	An insect ...
Hood	That ...

David   Hunts other insects …
Hood   It is called praying mantis because …
David   It has two big feelers and it looks like it's praying.
Hood   Good. Tell me again.
David told me the start another couple of times. Each time he seemed to have more confidence.
Hood   Now, do you think you could write it?
David   I think so.

David managed this quite well. I had to go back and discuss 'What sort of insects does it eat,' and later, 'How does it catch them?' David had a lot of information, but his first reaction was that it was 'boring'.

Why was this task boring to David? Let us consider the reasons.
1. There was no purpose. Who was he writing for? Who was the audience? It was obviously seen as writing for the teacher.
2. The teacher gave him an inappropriate form. 'Beginning, middle and end' are used in the writing of narrative.
3. David had not been instructed on the form. He had no plan to work from. He had disorganised notes and no structure.
4. As David had few, if any, strategies to attack the problem, he said the work was 'boring'.
5. The young teacher did not know what she was trying to teach, and so could not assess the learning needs of the child.

I believe that this is a good example of lack of teacher knowledge, and in her case, experience, which translated into learner frustration. It only requires one David in the classroom to disrupt the learning of others. So what should she have done?
1. Made sure the children knew the form by engaging them in the shared writing of a number of like pieces.
2. Made sure the children had a clear understanding of audience and purpose, e.g. 'The children in Room 8 know nothing about insects. Our book will help them find out what they want to know.'
3. Made sure that they had a planning method to sort and order information.
4. Identified children such as David who needed to be guided through the writing of this piece, paragraph by paragraph.

There is not enough thought put into supporting young writers as they learn how to write unfamilar forms. Potential problems needs to be identified. Ask:
- *Who can?* Turn them loose!
- *Who can, with help, be guided through the writing task? Who cannot?* Write the piece.

These approaches of course have been explored in some depth in the chapter 'Shared and Guided Writing.'

Mary's major problem was lack of knowledge. I have mentioned throughout this book that quality teacher in-service programmes are vital if quality writing programmes are going to develop. Teachers *cannot* be blamed for not teaching what they do not know, but school administrators *can* be blamed for not providing quality teacher-development programmes.

This brings us back to the issue of assessment. Quality assessment starts off by knowing and understanding each of the following.
- **What** to assess
- **When** to assess
- **Who** to assess
- **How** to assess
- **Why** to assess
- **Where** to assess.

In the next chapter assessment is examined in greater detail.

> **Some Key Conclusions**
>
> The rapid change that has taken place in the curriculum in recent years has placed enormous pressures on teachers. The pace of change has been too great.
>
> The New Zealand English Curriculum has been affected by competing philsophies. The result is a document which makes it very difficult for teachers to interpret what they are being asked to teach.
>
> There is a belief that children need to be able to control the three types of writing: expressive, poetic, and transactional. However, very little writing is purely one of these three.
>
> It is essential that teachers fully understand the different writing forms.

8

In this chapter

- Monitoring the individual
- Learning characteristics during three stages of development
- A junior school vision
- Assessing curriculum programmes
- Levels One to Four outcomes

Monitoring the Individual – Assessing the Curriculum

Teachers have to assess the curriculum as set out by their educational authority. Although the 'powers that be' make all the right noises about 'assessing and meeting individual needs', if the curriculum statements are not being measured, the school is in for a tough time. Currently, teachers are being asked to assess curriculum programmes and at the same time monitor the writing strategies of the individual. Let's examine these tasks.

Monitoring the Individual

The teacher is charged with monitoring the progress of the individual. Teachers need to know these things about the learner.
- The child's attitude towards writing.
- The child's spelling ability.
- The child's control over a range of print concepts.
- The child's control over a range of genres.
- The child's ability to use a range of writing strategies – planning, proofreading, revision and publishing.

There are a number of ways the teacher may monitor the progress of the individual. In this section I would like to explore some of the available options.

Why monitor?

First, why monitor? Most teachers would list the following reasons:
- To review prior teaching.
- To report to our colleagues.
- To report to parents.
- For the funding body.

Often the one item that is missing is *reporting to the child*. The child has, or should have, the greatest stake in the venture. Too often the child is never told what they know or what they are expected to learn. As mentioned elsewhere in this book, the teaching agenda is often kept a secret.

Our philosophy as writers of *Dancing with the Pen* was that the teacher must first concentrate on what the pupil can do, not what the pupil cannot do. Most of our teaching in the past has been so negative that finding the deficiencies is second nature to most teachers. After all, it is the way most people were taught, and it is human nature to endeavour to repeat one's own experiences. Having to look at what the writer can do makes teachers think in a different direction. I would contend this is the most valuable data a teacher can gather because, having focused on the positive aspects of the writing behaviour, it is possible to make an informed teaching decision.

The portfolio

Samples of the child's writing give insight into how the child writes. Draft samples are of far more interest than published work. The draft is the 'early in the morning' face. The published piece is dressed up for an evening out. It is hard to realise they are the same pieces of writing.

Samples collected over a number of months are of great interest to the teachers of writing. They should show the pupil's growth as a writer. Why keep a sample that shows nothing new? In this respect the teacher needs to have some criteria for observation. The Learning

Learning Characteristics During Three Stages of Development

Characteristics of the Emergent Writer
- I display writing like behaviours (these may not be words).
- I am establishing principles of directionality.
- I am learning about the spaces between words.
- I am learning how to orient a page.
- I am learning how to hold a pencil.
- I am developing consistency of letter form.
- I am learning how to spell some words.
- I can locate some words in the class.
- I am developing some knowledge of letters/sounds.
- I am learning to use the teacher's models as a basis for writing.
- I can explain orally the meaning of my pictures.
- My title is linked to my writing.
- I am starting to ask questions about other people's writing.
- I can talk to others about my writing.
- I expect my teacher to help me with my writing.
- Although my attempts at spelling are semi-phonetic in form, my writing can be read by others.

Learning Characteristics During Three Stages of Development

Characteristics of the Early Writer
- I read over my writing to check meaning.
- I can talk freely about my topic.
- I can use a sound sequencing strategy to make logical spelling attempts.
- I have started to identify my attempts at spelling.
- I am starting to self-correct some of these.
- I am extending the number of words I can spell accurately.
- I am starting to use a number of print conventions, e.g. capital letters, fullstops, etc.
- I am able to make some corrections to surface features.
- While I may have difficulty in keeping to the topic, I can see the need to try.
- I am selecting from a wider range of topics.
- I am able to sustain a piece of writing over several days.
- I enjoy taking part in shared writing activities.
- I am experimenting with different genres.
- I am confident that I have the skills and abilities to express my thoughts quickly and efficiently in a written form.

Characteristics of the Fluent Writer
- I can write using simple sentence forms.
- I am starting to try to use more complex sentences.
- I can write in a variety of forms for a variety of purposes. I know my audience and this influences my written form.
- I use the skills of the writing process in all areas of the curriculum.
- I am developing a range of study skills that help me locate and order information.
- I can use brainstorming and note-taking as a strategy to gain information about a topic.
- I am learning to plan, develop and sequence my ideas.
- I am starting to try to set out my work in paragraphs and chapters.
- I use a variety of ways to lead into my writing, I know I can experiment with these.
- I am starting to build plot, characters, settings, suspense and climax into my narrative writing.
- I understand how to revise and am demonstrating a range of these strategies.
- I can use alternative language to improve my text.
- I am developing a growing control over a wide range of surface features.
- My proofreading of my work is becoming habitual.
- I have sound dictionary skills and apply these during proofreading.
- I can use the language of the writer.
- I can publish my work in a variety of ways.
- I can use a variety of illustrating styles in keeping with the purpose of the writing.
- I do not process all my work. Purpose will dictate the degree of processing required.

Characteristics lists provided here allow a child to be placed within a developmental band. The teacher should take a sample of the pupil's writing and note on the bottom key information about what the child is able to do. It should also indicate an area for development. These samples are useful for reporting to parents.

Most parents want to know where their child is succeeding. They also want to know what the school is doing to further his development. As a parent I would be really pleased to get this data in a report.

Earlier in the book I mentioned the use of the *I Can* and *I Am Learning* lists. These have not been well used. The problem is that most teachers fall behind in maintaining them. They leave them and then try to bring thirty lists up to date at once. Teachers should focus on reviewing eight lists a week. In this way, every month each child's list will be maintained.

Sample books

Some schools send home sample books once a month. This is a great way to maintain on-going reporting. The danger is that the work done in the sample books often does not reflect the usual day-to-day work in class.

A friend of mine took over a small school and inherited a sample book programme. He had the children do their normal day's work in the book on the last Friday of the month. After the second month an irate parent arrived at the school complaining that his child's work had deteriorated since my friend had become his teacher. 'He could spell before you came,' was the parent's complaint.

Of course, what had happened was my friend had been sending home samples of draft writing. The previous teacher only sent home published work. Teachers must be sure they know what information they are trying to communicate to their parents. I believe at times these books can be quite misleading.

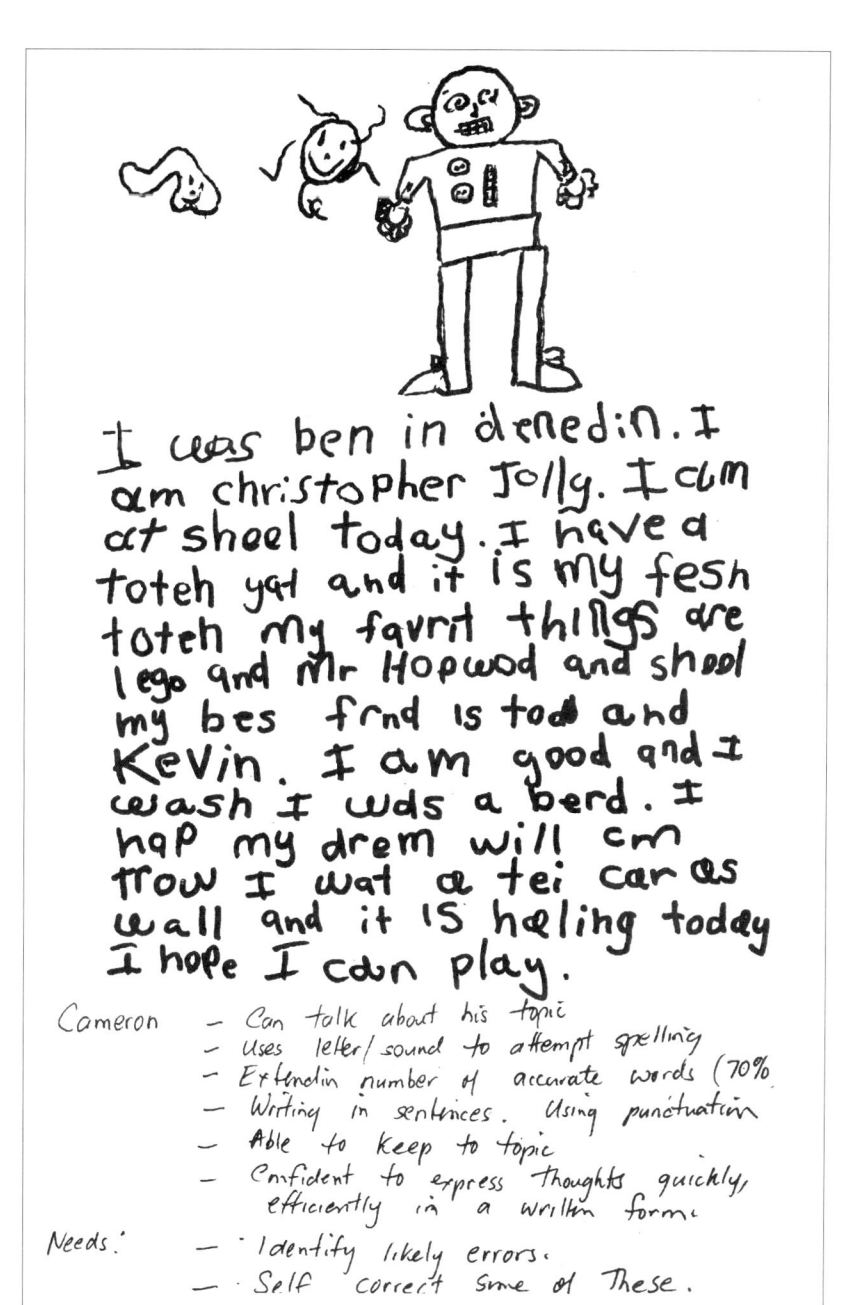

> I was ben in denedin. I am christopher Jolly. I cum at shool today. I have a toteh yat and it is my fesh toteh my favrit things are lego and Mr Hopwod and shool my bes frnd is tod and Kevin. I am good and I wash I wds a berd. I hap my drem will cm trow I wat a tei car as wall and it is heling today I hope I can play.
>
> Cameron
> — Can talk about his topic
> — Uses letter/sound to attempt spelling
> — Extending number of accurate words (70%)
> — Writing in sentences. Using punctuation
> — Able to keep to topic
> — Confident to express thoughts quickly, efficiently in a written form.
>
> Needs:
> — Identify likely errors.
> — Self correct some of these.

(Teacher's comment)
Christopher Jolly

Christopher is able to express his thoughts quickly and efficiently in a written form. He is able to write a number of words accurately and can make logical attempts at spelling unknown words using letter–sound matching. He is able to use capital letters and punctuate using fullstops. He enjoys writing, and writes honestly, expressing a range of feelings.

His next task is to learn to identify likely spelling errors and make an attempt at correcting some of the easier words that he should now be learning to spell.

▲ The above example shows how a teacher might analyse a sample of a pupil's writing and the key information that might be recorded.

The interview
I have found the best way to gather data is to 'ask the patient'. If children can explain how they work and how they think, teachers can better help them. I regularly ask children questions such as:
- Do you plan your work?
- What ways could you plan?
- How do you attempt to spell a word you are unsure of?
- Do you proofread your work?
- What does the teacher expect you to be able to correct?
- What do you do when you come across a word you don't know?
- What part of writing do you like best?
- What part do you like least?
- What is the teacher teaching you to do in writing at the moment?
- Do you like writing?

These interviews tell the researcher a lot about the classroom programme. They also are useful for the classroom teacher. Self-reflection is probably the best form of assessment a teacher can engage in.

Checklists, charts and graphs
Any system that confronts a child with a great list of things that must be checked off is probably of little use to the learner. I well remember Donald Graves talking about the child who said 'One down, ninety-two to go!'

Checklists can be useful for the teacher in that they give information on which to base observations, but in my opinion they are quite useless to the learner. Checklists may also have value in terms of a school's cumulative record system.

In these times schools are charged with monitoring the child against national curriculum objectives. I have given a range of outcomes later in this chapter to help teachers make these observations more reliable. Without such a system, monitoring curriculum objectives may involve a lot of guesswork. It is important that schools have a system that shows where the child is currently working, and that progress made during a year's instruction can be monitored. In saying this I believe that graphs and charts must be made simple enough so that a teacher can complete the assessment task quickly and easily. This final marking off should be based on the sum total of the collected data.

The thing to always remember is that if the data is not useful, why collect it? If nothing 'wearable' is going to come out of all the time spent on 'measuring the cloth', why hire a tailor? Often systems are overlaid on top of systems. I would suggest that schools select the ones that are useful to them and try to make one assessment, keeping the data in one place. They should not have to transfer data from one set of records to another and adding needlessly to their workload.

A Junior-School Vision
By the end of Year Three children will be able to do the following:
- Show they have a sound attitude towards writing.

- Know who they are writing for.
- Know their readers expect their questions to be answered.

By the end of Year Three children will have sufficient skills to:
- Write many known words.
- Have a method for attempting to spell unknown words.
- Make some attempt at correcting these.
- Have enough motor skill to write legibly.
- Be aware of the place of print conventions and be able to use a number of these accurately.
- Clarify meaning by adding to text.

They will be able to write in several forms – namely, retell personal experience, tell simple narrative stories and write simple letters. They will have experienced the satisfaction of seeing their voice in print.

A vision such as this one above gives us something on which to base our programmes. Children will meet these challenges and gain these skills at different rates. Some will move in excess of this list by the end of their third year, while others will still be striving to achieve this list by the time they complete Year Six. While the teacher has an overall vision, the needs of each child will be different.

Assessing Curriculum Programmes

So, what is so difficult in measuring curriculum statements? Usually they are very broad and do not set out specific learning outcomes. I have already pointed out in the previous chapter some of the problems of interpreting the intentions of the English statement. As has been shown, the New Zealand curriculum is very wordy and open to a variety of interpretations.

In this section, the achievement objectives for the written language strand of the English Curriculum are analysed and a set of learning outcomes suggested for Levels One to Four (Years One to Eight).

LEVEL 1 (Approximate age band 5–7 years)

EXPRESSIVE
Students should:
- *write spontaneously to record personal experiences.*

Developmental Path
Label
E.g. *'I am going to Grandma's house.'*
(The writer adds a statement under an illustration)

Observation and Comment
E.g. *'I am going to Grandma's house because she had been sick.'* (Often these comments are added at the end – *'it was cool fun'*. The use of words such as 'but' and 'because' by very young writers seem to indicate writing ability.)

Recount
E.g. *'Yesterday I went to Grandma's to help her with the washing. I don't like wet sheets. Grandma gave me a drink of lime but I don't like lime so I gave it to the cat. It sniffed it and went outside. Then I went home.'* (See section in Chapter 6 on transactional writing for an explanation of the differences between 'expressive' and 'transactional' recounts.) Children will also experiment with notes, simple letters to friends, lists, etc.

POETIC
Students should:
- *write on a variety of topics, beginning to shape ideas.*

Label
The label from a drawing.
E.g. *'My dog is chasing the rabbit.'*

Observation and Comment
E.g. *'My dog chased the rabbit. It caught it. It was horrible.'*

The Fictionalisation
E.g. *'My dad took me rabbit hunting. We were chased by a big bear. Dad had to shoot it.'* (This is fictionalised because of the way the writer *wished* it had happened.)

Retell
E.g. *'Once upon a time there was a girl called Little Red Riding Hood.'* (Moving from first-person storyteller rather than participant.)

TRANSACTIONAL

Students should:
- *write instruction and recount events in authentic contexts.*

There are two key considerations here. First, instructions – What should be expected from children of this age? Second, the recount – how is the transactional recount different to the expressive recount?

Instructions
Awareness of a process.

Label
E.g. *'I am making a cake.'*

Observation and Comment
'I am making a cake. It has flour in it.'
With adequate shared writing experiences, there comes an understanding that some texts tell people how to do things. Teachers must also try to ensure there is a close link with the reading programme. As children meet procedural text during their reading, links across to the writing of this genre should be established.

Level 1 instructions should be processes that children can observe over a short timespan. Donald Graves talks of 'short-term data-gathering'. This is where activities such as giving instructions as how to cross a road, eat a banana or make a cup of coffee give children real contexts for writing. Examples such as the above are:
- Easily observed.
- Have very few steps.
- Can be easily pictorially recorded (planned).
- Are easily translated into written text.

The danger is that teachers may try to get too complex too soon. An example of Level One instructions: *How to Eat a Banana:*
1. Get the banana.
2. Peel the banana.
3. Eat the banana.
4. Throw the skin in the rubbish bin.

The Recount
The developmental path for transactional recounting is the same as for expressive recounting. So why differentiate? The difference is in *purpose*. If the reason for recounting is to *inform*, it is *transactional*. If it is to talk about the *feelings and impressions* left by the experience, it is *expressive*.

An Example of a Transactional Recount
E.g. *'Last Wednesday afternoon we went to Davidson's butcher shop to see Mr Davidson make sausages. When we arrived Mr Davidson showed us the big mincer where all the meat is minced up. He then showed where the oatmeal and other things that go into sausages are kept. Mr Davidson let Tom put bits of meat in the machine ….'*

The purpose is not to tell the reader about personal feelings, and how the writer felt about the experience; the purpose is essentially to recount information. Quite often expressive and transactional recounting may become mixed. Over a period of years, the writer develops a clear idea of *audience* and *purpose*. Teachers must start this development at Level 1 by encouraging the writer to state *why* they are writing and *who* they are writing for.

Explanations
Level 1 children can also write explanations. Teachers lead children into this by suggesting a topic that is expressed as a question.
E.g. *'Why is it frosty in Winter?'*
'In winter it gets all frosty. Jack Frost comes with a spray can and sprays it white.'

While giving children opportunity to explain, teachers should not expect these attempts to be scientifically accurate.

LEVEL 1 Expected Generic Learning Outcomes

What to write
The writer will:
- initially use drawings to plan and generate ideas

- increase planning options by discussing with friends, using picture webs

- through shared writing experience, children will be exposed to word/picture webs, word webs and phrase webs used to record sequences of time

- initially lack technical skills, so first recounts may well be oral. As skills such as spelling develop, detail will increase

- through guided writing attempt to use picture webs and discussion to write personal recounts, transactional recounts and re-tellings

- link ideas in recounts using time words such as 'and' and 'then'.

How to write
The writer will:
- use featured vocabulary to construct stylised sentences. These will include the use of a range of sentence starters based around words such as 'I am', 'Here is', and 'We are going'. These will likely reflect use of present and future tense and develop knowledge of the alphabet

- use this knowledge to link letter names to sounds in making logical attempts at spelling unknown words

- use an underlining method to indicate likely spelling errors

- make attempts at self-correction of some errors that are close to being visually correct

- be able to write a growing number of high-frequency words

- develop a limited written vocabulary of interest words.

How to construct
The writer will:
- understand the differences between words and letters

- through shared writing experiences be shown the link between thinking in sentences and writing in sentences

- through shared writing experiences be exposed to a range of print conventions such as capital letters (names and start of sentence), fullstops, question marks, exclamation marks, speech marks.

The audience
The writer will:
- understand the importance of information such as title, author and illustrator to the reader

- share work with teacher, neighbour and with class

- attempt to answer questions about the writing

- through shared writing, see that ideas can be added on and into text to clarify meaning

- through shared writing be exposed to the idea that different forms of writing are used for different purposes

- through shared writing be made aware that different audiences expect writing to be presented in different ways.

The product
The writer will:
- learn conventions of publication. Terms such as *title, author* and *illustrator* will be used and understood when discussing published work

- through publication, discover that illustrations aid the reader

- publish material for a variety of audiences

- expect a response from the audience

- expect to publish often.

LEVEL 2   (Approximate age band 7–9 years)

While Level 1 saw a natural development of a range of different types of writing, Level 2 requires more teacher-led development. Writers at this level should be given time to consolidate the learning that has already taken place. At the same time, teacher demonstration, through a variety of shared writing experiences, and the demands of the general curriculum, will extend the range of introduced genres.

EXPRESSIVE WRITING
The student should:
- *write regularly and spontaneously to record personal experiences and observations.*

The writer will:
- now be able to write quite fluently using an inventive spelling form
- recount experiences, making comments and observations of events
- write daily, being given time to consolidate their growing ability to construct written text
- through close reading be exposed to examples of diary writing
- be given opportunity to experiment with maintenance of a journal, log or diary
- through shared and guided writing, investigate a range of form poetry
- write letters to friends, pen friends
- write reminders, lists, notes.

Expressive Recount
E.g. Purpose: Recall events and make observations regarding feelings and thoughts.

'Last Sunday we went to Grandma's. I love going to Grandma's because she makes lovely scones. When we arrived, Grandma had just started baking. She asked me if I would like to help, so I rubbed the butter into the flour. I love the feel of butter as it runs through your fingers.'

POETIC WRITING
The student should:
- *write on a variety of topics, shaping ideas in a number of genres such as letters, poems and narratives, and making choices in language and form.*

Children will explore narrative structures through close reading of narrative texts. This will include identification of major features such as main and supporting characters, setting, problem and resolution and conclusion. Language exploration, looking at the use of adjectives in description, characters and settings will, hopefully, encourage children to experiment with these features as they engage in their own writing.

The writer will:
- engage in shared writing of narratives
- during shared and guided writing learn why writers construct flow charts or plot lines when planning narratives
- through shared and guided writing engage in exercises that involve writing description of setting and characters
- experiment in writing various narrative genres. These are likely to be based around their reading, and include examples of recalled language
- write letters designed to recount narrative to friends and acquaintances
- be exposed to, and experiment with, varieties of narrative poetry
- begin to make choices in terms of genre and language usage. These choices should be influenced by audience and purpose.

TRANSACTIONAL WRITING
Students should:
- *write instructions and explanations, state fact and opinions, and recount events in a range of authentic contexts.*

The writer will:
- write recounts to record information gathered during field trips and visits
- engage in shared and guided writing where the text features of both instruction and explanations are explained
- understand that instructions need a title and list of materials, and that reading is easier if there are spaces between each sentence
- write explanations describing the workings of simple household technology, e.g. kitchen grater, garlic crusher, egg beater and torch
- engage in shared and guided writing of factual reports. Topics might include recording information from visits to the supermarket, police, fire station, bakery and other places of general interest. Factual reports will also include simple research topics such as volcanoes, different varieties of bird, insects and animals
- understand that these reports have opening statements and paragraphs containing information
- give their opinions on issues of interest to the children, e.g. the length of school holidays, playground problems, advertising aimed at children – 'I believe that …'.

LEVEL 2 Expected Generic Learning Outcomes

What to write
The writer will:
- develop confidence in writing all the forms developed during Level 1

- through shared and guided writing be exposed to factual (third person) recounts, formal letter setting out, and the generic form of the narrative

- with assistance, question, research, sort, structure information reports, explanations, instructions. Through shared writing, the writer will be exposed to methods of planning narrative through the use of a plot line or flow chart in order to map out a simple narrative of character, setting, problem, resolution, conclusion

- with initial assistance, be able to plan using some of the following methods: drawing, picture webbing, discussing, key word of phrase webbing

- experiment with brainstorming and sorting

- with assistance, generate possible headings for sorting information during the writing of transactional texts

- understand instructions are easier to read if they contain a goal, list of materials, leave gaps between steps, have diagrams to assist meaning

- experiment with maintaining a daily diary/journal/log

- attempt to use writing across curriculum.

How to write
The writer will:
- extend vocabulary choices

- through shared writing meet a widening range of adjectives, and attempt to select from a range of more interesting, and exact, verbs and adjectives

- be able to operate at the transitional or 'correct' levels of spelling development

- continue to develop a system of error identification

- acquire a growing control over dictionary skills that will enable the writer to become more accurate in proofreading spelling

- be aware of the use of the thesaurus, and attempt to use this during writing

- have developed an extensive, accurate, written vocabulary, i.e. the accurate use of the most commonly used words contained in the English language.

How to construct
The writer will:
- experiment with a wide range of sentence starters

- attempt to use a variety of simple and more compound sentence forms

- understand the concept of paragraph. This will be especially true when developed through prior planning of factual texts where the headings provide the structure

- use a widening range of conventions such as capital letters (as at the start of a sentence, proper nouns), fullstops, comma, exclamation mark, speech marks, colon (when used in factual reports)

- use terms such as *draft, proofreading, revision* and *publish* when discussing the construction of text.

The audience
The writer will:
- identify the part audience plays when it comes to selecting form and register

- will share writing with a partner, class and teacher

- be confident in defending writing when faced with questions from the audience

- be more proficient in making choices based on audience and purpose. This still may require clarification through discussion

- show more consideration for the reader through accuracy of proofreading and quality of final product.

The product
The writer will:
- understand that not all work needs to be published

- show a shift from the egocentric reasons for publication to a more audience-driven desire to produce quality work

- publish in a variety of ways

- expect the audience to respond to writing when the meaning is not clear.

LEVEL 3   (Approximate age band 9–11 years)

EXPRESSIVE
Students should:
- *Write regularly and with ease to express personal responses to different experiences and to record observations and ideas.*

The children should now be used to the routine of keeping a daily diary and recording observations in learning logs and making jottings in daily journals.

They should also have acquired sufficient writing skill that spelling and punctuation have become habitual.

The expressive recount should now be showing development. The ability to not just record events, but 'focus down' on specific events enables the writer to be more specific. The writer will now be expected to respond to *elements* of the experience rather than communicate their global meaning. This should enable the writer to make more detailed observations and explore specific ideas.

The writer will:
- maintain a daily diary, explore the curriculum by writing regularly in a learning log, or by recording jottings in a learning journal
- use writing as a life skill, e.g. to make notes, lists, reminders
- understand how to lift out a segment of a recount plan and expand this to write only about a single aspect of an experience
- be willing to explore and comment on events, record feelings, and make observations on a range of experiences
- through shared writing be exposed to the concept that writers write to discover the *meaning* within the experience.

POETIC WRITING
Students should:
- *Write on a variety of topics, shaping, editing, and reworking texts in a range of genres and using vocabulary and convention, such as spelling and sentence structure, appropriate to the genre.*

At this level the writer will be familiar with the narrative structure. It is expected that a range of strategies will be employed as the writer plans the writing. There will be evidence that the writer understands the need to re-read and revise during the composition process. Through a range of close reading and shared writing experiences, children will be given opportunity to extend their vocabulary and see how language can be used for different purposes. The structural links between different forms of narrative will be starting to become apparent.

The writer will:
- through close reading and shared writing explore a range of narrative genres. These might include animal stories, adventure, fairy tale, legend, plays
- during close reading, discuss common elements found in different narrative genres and attempt to use these during their own writing
- through shared and guided writing, explore varieties of narrative poetry
- attempt to write simple plays. These may be group writing tasks
- make and use language choices, e.g. adjectives in description in an effort to enhance the writing, and extend the ability to self-edit work
- understand reasons for prior planning and be able to use a variety of strategies during rehearsal for writing
- through shared writing, be exposed to methods used by writers to describe characters, settings, feelings and relationship between characters
- through shared writing see how writing can be revised by adding to, adding into, reordering and deletion
- through shared writing investigate the place of real life experience in the construction of

narrative. The writer should be invited to contrast these with the stereotypical as a means of judging quality writing

- use the thesaurus to explore word options during revision
- use simple and compound sentence forms.

TRANSACTIONAL WRITING
Students should:
- *Write instructions, explanations and factual accounts and express personal viewpoints in a range of authentic contexts, sequencing ideas logically.*

The writer should now be able to understand the key elements of purpose and audience. The writer needs to be exposed to real events that both interest the learner and encourage investigation. The provision of an outside audience should encourage processing and publication. At times classroom writing tasks will only be used as an aid to recall. These pieces will probably be left in draft form. Whatever the case, the writer needs to clearly understand the purpose and audience in relation to the task.

The writer will:
- understand the text structure used for written instructions. This will be shown through the use of a heading, objective, lists of materials, action verbs at the start of sentences, gaps between each element, and diagrams as an aid to comprehension
- understand the structure of written explanations, and use these in the curriculum areas of technology and science
- be able to research, organise information, and structure factual reports on topics such as places of interest, people with interesting occupations and studies of animal or bird life
- through shared and guided writing investigate 'historical recounting' and its place in social studies
- through close reading come to understand the structure of factual recounts when used in newspaper reporting. Attempt to use this form when recording classroom and school events
- be able to express a written viewpoint on issues that are important to the class, school, or communities in which the writer lives
- through close reading explore arguments written in letters to the editor or newspaper editorials. Discuss structure, language use, effectiveness of arguments
- through shared and guided writing investigate the text structure of written argument, thesis, evidence and conclusion. See the need to consider, and counter, the other side of the case when constructing a written argument.

LEVEL 3 Expected Generic Learning Outcomes

What to write
The writer will:
- consolidate the writing forms developed during Levels 1 and 2 and be introduced to an extension of factual recounting, i.e. newspaper reporting, and to the structure of written argument

- understand that audience and purpose drive form and process

- know how to brainstorm, gather and sort information

- be able to generate headings for sorting information during transactional writing

- see purpose in setting questions for investigation, and use a range of study skills in order to locate answers to questions

- through shared and guided writing be exposed to strategies involving note-taking and summarising

- be able to choose from a number of planning methods when organising information

- be able to construct plot lines and flow charts when pre-planning narratives

- show an understanding of the structure of narrative and apply this to the development of different pieces of work

- be conversant with the method of setting out instructions and understand the place of diagrams

- become fluent when writing in a diary, learning log or journal

- become aware of the place of writing within the curriculum.

How to write
The writer will:
- see reason for using adjectives in narrative, verbs in instructions, emotive verbs in argument

- be correct in form (if not always accurate) in spelling attempts

- have a systematic method of identification and correction of errors

- be aware of elements of language such as common prefixes and suffixes, antonyms, synonyms, simile and metaphor

- be quick and efficient when using a dictionary. Use dictionary skills such as 'fanning', locating key words, and being able to open the dictionary close to the desired part of the alphabet

- make use of the thesaurus during revision of writing

- show evidence of a widening written vocabulary.

How to construct
The writer will:
- show evidence of varying the use of sentence starters

- use a variety of simple and compound sentences

- understand the need for every speaker to be recorded on a new line

- regularly use paragraphing in transactional text and start to carry this on into poetic and expressive writing

- habitually use print conventions such as capitalisation, fullstop, comma, exclamation mark, question mark, speech marks, colon (in transactional reports)

- understand the need to revise and apply a range of these strategies when writing

- use a meta-language when discussing the process of writing

- show an understanding of the terms: plan, draft, audience, revise, proofread and publish.

The audience
The writer will:
- share draft writing with: group, partner, class and teacher

- be confident in defending writing when faced with questions

- consider the audience when making decisions about writing. Show evidence of this through self-revision of aspects of draft writing.

The product
The writer will:
- show evidence of becoming self-critical when discussing a piece of writing. This will require the writer to not only identify that a piece of writing is good, but also attempt to describe its qualities

- identify how a piece might be improved, and how this might be accomplished

- be selective in picking a method of publication that meets the requirements of the audience and suits the game

- expect both positive and critical feedback of published work.

LEVEL 4   (Approximate age band 11–13 years)

EXPRESSIVE WRITING
Students should:
- *Write regularly and with ease to express personal responses to a range of experiences and texts, explore ideas and record observations.*

Writers should now have the technical skills to be able to write in order to reflect on aspects of their lives, their learning, what they have viewed, heard and read. They will be able to use written language as a tool to communicate what they know, as well as discover the meanings held within their experiences. Writing will not only be used as a tool of learning, but also one of self-discovery.

The writer should show proficiency in maintaining a diary, in note-taking, as well as jotting down ideas and reminders. The writer will hopefully carry these skills and abilities outside the classroom and use them in everyday life.

The writer will:
- explore ideas within an experience. 'How did this experience influence my life?' 'Why is this place important to me?' 'How have these events and people shaped the way I think?'
- will focus on an aspect of an experience and also attempt to investigate the meaning within. (This will need a lot of explaining during shared writing. Only a few children may see relevance and be able to operate in this manner)
- respond to the writings of others, expressing their feelings and thoughts on what they have read, seen or heard
- understand the ways close friends and acquaintances may influence the writer and the process of writing, e.g. the 'one off' nature of the writing often leads to superficial proofreading and editing
- show an awareness of style and personal voice when reviewing the work of professional writers, e.g. 'Even without looking at the name of the author, how would you know this was probably written by Margaret Mahey? Can you relate this to your own writing?'
- understand why readers require accuracy of spelling and punctuation.

POETIC WRITING
Students will:
- *Write on a variety of topics, shaping and reworking texts in a range of genres, expressing ideas and experiences imaginatively, and using appropriate vocabulary and conventions such as spelling and sentence structure.*

The writer will now be able to select from and write in a number of narrative genres. These structures should now be second nature to the writer and will enable experimentation with form, e.g. starting with the problem instead of setting the scene. The writer will also be experimenting with playwriting, both for stage and video, and will show an understanding of the revision process. The advanced writer will now probably become openly demanding in requesting to use a wordprocessor.

The writer will:
- experiment with the narrative structure, looking at different starting points within the narrative
- increase the range of available narrative forms. These may include myth, legend, science fiction, stage and video play, as well as varieties of narrative poetry
- explore through close reading, aspects of style and voice
- engage in shared group writing of video and stage plays
- be aware of the need for description in both

scene and character, and use during writing
- use dialogue wisely during writing and show an understanding of the conventions in its use
- use personal experiences to construct imaginative narrative. This will require the writer to take an experience and develop a possible narrative plot. This will hopefully enable the writer to see that writing gains authenticity when the writer knows the topic
- show evidence of a developing ability to use language. Writing will likely include a range of similes, metaphors and possible, simple examples of imagery.

TRANSACTIONAL WRITING
Students should:
- *Write instructions and factual accounts and express and explain a point of view in a range of authentic contexts, organising and linking ideas logically and making language choices appropriate to the audience.*

The writer should now be able to use a range of study skills when gathering and ordering information. Being able to recall much of what has been observed and back these with field notes enhances the quality of the writing. The use of specific scientific and technical language should give added authenticity to the language. The writer should be expected to investigate and use specific aspects of writing, e.g. the recount, in everyday life.

The writer will:
- be proficient in not only writing instructions, but in explaining text structure and linguistic form
- be proficient in writing explanations in science and technology, and be able to explain the textual and linguist structures involved
- be able to blend instructional and explanatory texts to record scientific experiments
- understand the place of recounting in everyday writing as found in the writing of police reports, accident reports, newspaper and sport reports. These should be explored in terms of language choice and usage
- be critical when comparing written records of the same event made by different writers
- be able to explain how audience and purpose has influenced the writing
- be able to state a point of view on items of interest. These may be important to the individual, class, community and possibly country. The writer should be required to back these with examples of fact and opinion
- engage in further shared and guided writing of arguments. The reason for engaging in these exercises is to teach the writer the need to produce evidence to counter any opposition case
- through shared and guided writing discover the differences between argument and discussion
- be able to use writing across the curriculum and to be selective in form, structure and language choices appropriate to the task and the audience. This will cover all forms that have been developed through Levels 1 to 4.

LEVEL 4 — Expected Generic Learning Outcomes

What to write
The writer will:
- be able to rationalise purpose, audience and choice of genre when selecting topic

- select, according to audience and purpose, a suitable method of planning and organising information

- confidently apply a range of study skills to the task of gathering and ordering information. These will include question setting, resource selection, use of index systems, skim-reading, note-taking, summarising, use of electronic resources, e.g. CD-ROM, interviewing, viewing, selecting and comparing

- demonstrate an ability to set up independent research projects and follow these through to written conclusions

- understand the need for prior planning of narrative texts. Use plot synopsis, flow charts, character outlines

- have a clear understanding of the following forms of writing: recount, narrative instructions, explanations, argument

- consolidate forms of writing developed during Levels 1 to 3, and through shared and guided writing attempt to write argument and discussion

- maintain a diary, log or journal

- use writing as a tool of learning across the curriculum.

How to write:
The writer will:
- be able to use and record direct speech, in appropriate ways

- understand conventions used in playwriting

- understand the main structures used in writing advertisements

- have and use a range of strategies in order to revise text

- apply the process of writing to any writing task

- use a systematic method of error identification and self-correction

- show proficiency in use of dictionary and thesaurus

- demonstrate a respect for the reader by being accurate in spelling when publishing

- develop an ever-widening lexicon of known words.

How to construct
The writer will:
- be able to use a variety of sentence structures, including simple, compound and complex sentences

- understand simple sentence structure, including place of nouns, adjectives, adverbs and their relationships with the syntax of language

- understand the use of adverbial and adjectival phrases within sentence structure

- be able to rationalise making appropriate language choices

- show an awareness of, and attempt to use, antonyms, synonyms, metaphor, simile, personification, alliteration

- understand the use of common prefixes and suffixes

- engage in word study when words contain common elements. Some examples could include the following: cent, scribe, bio, auto, audio, deci, multi-, bio, equi-, bene, mal-, micro, trans, scope, contra, port (to name but a few)

- use a variety of sentence starters

- be proficient in the use of paragraphs.

The audience
The writer will:
- share drafts with group, partner, class and teacher

- engage in self-conferencing in order to predict, and thus avoid, likely questions

- be able to rationalise actions taken during writing, and defend a point of view

- consistently consider the importance of the reader during all stages of the writing process.

The product
The writer will:
- show pride in the finished product, and exhibit a willingness to think ahead to new projects

- seek critical feedback during all stages of the writing process

- be self-critical in order to improve current and future pieces of work

- be able to compare pieces done over a period of time and give a reasoned assessment of their quality

- understand the place of published versus draft writing in terms of purpose and audience

- use a variety of methods to pass information to a reader, including **written–oral, written,** and **written–visual** methods of publication.

9

In this chapter

- **Conclusions**

The Longest Journey

In gathering data for this book I have had the privilege of working with many teachers and many children throughout New Zealand. The one thing that has amazed me is the high interest in writing shown by teachers and children when I have visited them in their schools and classrooms. Teachers and schools must be congratulated on the way they have developed student interest in written language. So many children commented that they loved writing that their classroom writing experiences must therefore be viewed as being positive. However, in conclusion, there are a number of observations I would like to make about building on these positive features.

Conclusions

Once again the 1999 NEMP interviews with Year Four and Eight children show clearly that children consider the various narrative genres to be 'real' writing; they do not seem to understand the curriculum–writing links.

There seems to be clear evidence that children consider writing to be their choice or story, and do not see a cross-curricular link. In many cases older children are publishing only two or three pieces during a three-month instructional period. This is because they equate length with quality. I believe there is a need to encourage children to attempt more short, cross-curricular pieces of writing. In doing so, children will move at a faster pace through the process. The more pieces they process, the more skills they will acquire.

Children do not have clear goals for proofreading. Most children I have interviewed discussed generalities and were not specific about what they had to do. Many were also not clear as to what the teacher's responsibilities were when editing.

Generally, proofreading standards among older children can be improved. Often, the length of the piece does not encourage children to attempt the donkey-work of proofreading. In many cases the tasks set are not realistic, so children do not spend much time locating mistakes.

It has been pleasing to see that most children can verbalise strategies used when attempting to spell unknown words. Most seem to use a sound-related strategy while a few use a visual spelling method. A great number of children have clearly been well taught to 'sound it out, underline, check in a dictionary later'. The ability to articulate their strategies can teach us a lot about how children think.

There are still, however, a number of teachers who are tied to the concept of first-time accuracy. Often their children say, 'I write it on a piece of paper and take it to the teacher. She will spell it properly for me.' There is also another group of children who remain keen to pass over total responsibility to the teacher. 'I guess the first letter, then put a line. She will do the rest.'

It is clear that the question of spelling accuracy, self-correction, and the place of *Exploring Language* within the writing programme must be addressed. This has been covered quite extensively in this revised text.

The 1999 NEMP tests have strengthened my belief that insufficient work is being done to demonstrate the place of revision within the writing process. Many children seem to think of revision in terms of proofreading or editing. It is often not until the end that children are encouraged to ask, 'Does it make sense?' alongside the instruction 'Correct the spelling and the punctuation.' I believe that meaning always comes first and that children must be encouraged to continually reread their work as they write. Spelling and punctuation are mechanics and should be viewed as separate parts of the overall process. It must also be remembered that writing has a meta-language of its own. There is a need for teachers to be sure of using accurate terminology when discussing writing with their students.

Individual and class goal-setting must still be a concern. My 1994 research showed that few children actually understood what they were expected to learn. Teachers must consider whether students have clear learning goals and objectives. I am sure teachers are quite clear in what they are trying to achieve, but this needs to be more clearly communicated to the learners.

I feel some concern that children seem to still view the teacher as the major audience for their writing. While this is probably realistic in that writing is being done in a classroom situation, I believe that general low levels of child publication, as well as poor production standards, play a part in fostering this belief. Although most children I have worked with could identify someone as a reader, I wonder if children have clear purposes and audiences in mind as they write.

There are several areas of concern that are going to have to be addressed. First, the gender question. In the 1999 NEMP tests, girls out-performed boys in more than 80 per cent of the tasks. In general, they wrote better, had better attitudes about writing, and achieved at a greater level of competency than their male counterparts. The whole area of male literacy needs wider investigation.

Second, the matter of differences between schools in more advantaged areas and their less affluent cousins must be looked at. It seems to me that the rich are getting richer, the poor poorer, in education as well as in everyday life. Something must be done to provide some sort of equity.

Next, the ongoing problems of Maori education require serious attention. The NEMP research revealed that at Year Four Maori boys had a very positive view of writing; by Year Eight this had dissipated. What is the reason for this? Is it because writing becomes so closely matched to the curriculum that if they are not succeeding in the content areas they will not succeed in writing? Success breeds success, and many of these children are viewing themselves as educational failures. This must not be allowed to continue.

Finally, the problems children face leaving primary school and moving into the secondary school system must be addressed.

Recently I had the pleasure of spending two days observing a variety of subjects being taught within a boys' college. It became very evident to me that unless they could read and write adequately, many children were wasting their time at school. Subjects such as mathematics and science have a high language content. If learners can't comprehend the text, they are in trouble. One teacher showed me the 1998 School Certificate geography exam. It required the student to read thirty-five pages of text as well as answer the questions!

The secondary schools blame the intermediates; the intermediates the primaries; the primaries the homes. Literacy *is* a society problem. Educationalists talk of the *a-literate* child. This child can read, but won't. Children are not acquiring quality language because they are not exposed to it. One does not learn language from a TV set! One does not learn to read by playing video games.

There is just so much to do. Mao said, 'The longest journey starts with the first step.' I believe we have taken the first step. Now is the time to carry on and complete the journey.

Appendix One: Conditions for Learning

Outlined below are the necessary conditions in which children best learn to write according to the authors C. Cambourne and D. Graves.

CAMBOURNE	GRAVES
IMMERSION	• Child works in a writing environment rich in models of different forms of writing. • Child writes with a purpose.
DEMONSTRATION	• Teacher writes with the children. • Teacher shows the process in action. • Teacher writes pieces of work with children.
EXPECTATION	• Teacher must believe all children capable of writing. • Teacher expects independent writing from the first day of school.
RESPONSIBILITY	• Child has responsibility to draw ideas from models. • Child must integrate new knowledge. • Child must have input into topic choice.
APPROXIMATION	• Child must take risks. • Child must write without assistance. • Child can use 'invented spelling'. • Child must write and revise drafts.
EMPLOYMENT	• Child must take part in daily writing. • Child must plan use of time. • Child must use a similar process across all subject areas.
FEEDBACK	• Child must gain responses from audiences.

Select Bibliography

Ashton-Warner, S. (1980), *Teacher*, Virago, London.
Bissex, G. (1980), *Gnys at Wrk: a child learns to read and write*, Cambridge, Massachusetts: Harvard University Press.
Clay, M.M. (1973), *What Did I Write?*, Auckland: Heinemann.
Calkins, L.M. (1991), *Living Between the Lines*, Portsmouth: Heinemann.
Calkins, L.M. (1986), *Lessons From a Child*, Portsmouth: Heinemann.
Calkins, L.M. (1983), *The Art of Teaching Writing*, Portsmouth: Heinemann.
Cambourne, B. (1988), *The Whole Story*, Auckland: Ashton Scholastic.
Croft, C. (1998), *Spel Write*, NZCER Distribution Services, NZ.
Daly, E. (ed.) (1990), *Monitoring Children's Language Development*, Melbourne: Australian Reading Association.
Dalton, J. (1985), *Adventures in Thinking: creative thinking and co-operative learning in small groups*, Melbourne: Thomas-Nelson.
De Ath, P. (1993), *You Can Spell*, Longman Paul.
Derewiaka, B. (1990), *Exploring How Text Works*, Sydney: Primary English Teaching Association.
Dickson, D. (1988), *Write from the Start: a tool kit for young writers*, Melbourne: Macmillan.
Gentry, R. (1987), *Spel is a Four-Letter Word*, Scholastic.
Gentry, J.R. (1982), 'An Analysis of Developmental Spelling in GNYS AT WRK' in *The Reading Teacher*, pp. 192–9.
Graves, D. (1994), *A Fresh Look at Writing*, USA: Heinemann.
Graves, D. (1983), *Writing: teachers and children at work*, Exeter, New Hampshire: Heinemann.
Heenan, J. (1986), *Writing: Process and Product: a guide to classroom programmes*, Auckland: Longman Paul.
Hervey, S. (1995), *Linking Oral and Written Language*, Dunedin College of Education.
Hood, H.R. (1986), 'Finding the Swan in the Ugly Duckling', in *Forum*, New Zealand Reading Association, No. 1.
Meek, M. (1982), *Learning to Read*, London: The Bodley Head.
Ministry of Education (1991), *Dancing with the Pen*, Wellington; Learning Media.
Ministry of Education (1995), *English in the New Zealand Curriculum*.
Ministry of Education (1996), *Exploring Language*.
Mooney, M. (1987), *Developing Life-long Readers*, Department of Education, Wellington.
Murray, D. (1982), *Learning by Teaching: selected articles*, Upper Montclair: Boynton-Cook.
NEMP (1999), *Writing Report*, Otago University Research Unit/Ministry of Education.
Nicholson, T. (2000), *Reading the Writing on the Wall: debates, challenges and opportunities in the teaching of reading*, Palmerston North: Dunmore Press.
O'Rourke, A. and Philips, D. (1989), *Responding Effectively to Pupils' Writing*, New Zealand Council for Educational Research, Wellington.
Stewart-Dore, D. (ed.) (1986), *Writing and Reading to Learn*, Sydney: Primary English Teaching Association.
Ward, R.S. 1989, Group Conferences in Written Language with Older Children, *New Zealand Principal*, Vol. 1, No. 3.
Ward, R.S. and Cawkwell, G. (1991), Pupils Writing Out of School, *English in Aotearoa*, May–June, pp. 29–30.
Whitehead, D. (1998), *Catch them Thinking and Writing*, Arlington Heights, Il: Skylight Training and Publishing.
Wilson, R.G. (1974), *Creative Poetry*, RG Wilson Print.